FROM THE DARKNESS OF ADDICTION TO THE DAWN OF RECOVERY

A Practical Guide to Recovery For The Family Afflicted With Alcohol And Drug Addiction

by

Walter V. Lee & Chrystal M. Huey

Bloomington, IN
authorHOUSE®
Milton Keynes, UK

AuthorHouse™
1663 Liberty Drive, Suite 200
Bloomington, IN 47403
www.authorhouse.com
Phone: 1-800-839-8640

AuthorHouse™ UK Ltd.
500 Avebury Boulevard
Central Milton Keynes, MK9 2BE
www.authorhouse.co.uk
Phone: 08001974150

First published by AuthorHouse 6/12/2007

ISBN: 978-1-4343-0184-0 (sc)

Printed in the United States of America
Bloomington, Indiana

This book is printed on acid-free paper.

PARAPHRASE

--THREE LEVELS OF ADDICTION, THE DESTRUCTION OF THE FAMILY UNIT--

A TOTAL IN-DEPTH KNOWLEDGE OF ADDICTION, DRUGS, AND ALCOHOL WILL GIVE YOU

POWER OVER IT ALL

Most people that start using drugs and/or alcohol early in life usually do it because it's "all for fun", or the "in" thing to do, or "why not, mom and dad do it". If born into a family unit that is devastated with the use of drugs and or alcohol, we are already halfway to becoming addicted. During the early stage of life, birth to twelve years old, we learn about the use of drugs and alcohol from mom, dad, close family, and friends. A bad thing about this is that what we as children learn during the early stages of life is always right and never wrong when it comes from trusted and loved family and friends. To not believe those closest to us would not seem right. As we enter adolescence, we carry these negative skills and knowledge of drug and alcohol use right along with us into our teenage years. We have gotten more knowledgeable about how to use them. Of course we pass this knowledge on to other siblings and friends, trading information whenever possible. This passing around of information accumulates into a substantial bunch of misinformation. Children need taught the facts about drugs from a young age, so they would not be taught the wrong way later on in life.

By now, we know how to raise money and get the drugs. It often starts with stealing from mom and dad or other family members. The number one priority in life is not education or learning a skill. It is how to keep getting the drugs and alcohol, how to keep our high and not be caught. It is not long before our fund raising skills that kept us in drugs and alcohol need to grow beyond the boundaries of the home and family. We soon learn that stealing lawn mowers, bikes and many other small things can bring some fast cash. The conflicts at home escalate, in part, because of our behavior and may even get to the point of possible violence. We still cannot see how we can be so wrong. The people that are against our behavior are the parents that taught us this lifestyle. The bond with our family unit is strained to the breaking point. The bond we already had with our street friends usually becomes much stronger now. Our street friends may even become our new family unit.

By now, we are thrown into a lifestyle that is not ours by choosing. It is the only life we knew since birth and we are trying to make whatever we can out of it. To society, we are so wrong, but to us we are so very right. Most of us have a history with the law by now. We know what jail is because we have been in jail many times. Our family has disowned us and does not want us around anymore. We find ourselves keeping the tough guy look on the outside, but crying on the inside. We are starting to feel that maybe we are wrong but we do not know what to do about it. Our whole life has been a life of hell. We have seen other kids with good lives, seems like they are always happy and smiling. Suicidal thoughts are common now. We sure do not feel there is a God, because if there were, why would He make someone live like this. We find ourselves alone, cold, and hungry on a dark rainy night with nowhere to go and no place to call home. Soon we will be 18 years old.

This is the life for so many hundreds of thousands of children across this land right now. Many of us have lived this lifestyle and survived it by the grace of God. As the surviving adults of this lifestyle we can make the buck stop right here with us. We must not let our children live the same life we were forced to live and survive through. In most cases, the parents that passed this lifestyle on to their children were passing on the only lifestyle they knew. A lifestyle they were taught as children by their parents. There is one thing most of the children afflicted with this lifestyle have in common. Most of these children have never heard their parents say the words “I love you”.

Contents

CHAPTER 1

THERE ARE CHARTS THROUGHOUT THIS BOOK TO ILLUSTRATE WHAT YOU ARE READING ABOUT

INTRODUCTION

My Name is Walter V. Lee. I am an ADS Certified Licensed Rehabilitation Specialist. I have been working in the field of addiction rehabilitation since 1990. I started working as relief staff in the Shennum Center Detoxification Center in Concord, California and the East County Detoxification Center in Pittsburg, California while taking a full load of classes each semester in college. Working in the detoxification units, shelters, and missions is better known as "trench work". This is working with a part of our everyday life that most people would rather think does not exist. It is also known as the dark side of life. When I first started in this field in 1990, a lot of old timers believed strongly in the old way of doing things and were not about to let any change come in. At this time, the mental health services and addiction rehabilitation services had their own little silent war going on. As soon as some of these old timers could see I was about to change to a better way, many of them did not want me in the field. During the first five years of my working in this field, other staff persons accused me of many things. After I completed my college and received my certification, these attacks seemed to just stop. Once these old timers could see I was here to stay, they seemed to accept it.

While working in these detox units, I could see that the hopes and dreams of those in the bondage of addiction were no different from the hopes and dreams of the so-called "normal" people. The people that survive in this dark world of addiction are shut off from the rest of society. There seems to be the "them & us" mentality. I am a survivor of this darkened world I lived in for twenty- two years. I drank alcohol from dawn to dark, used many drugs I could get free, seven days a week. For years, I lived out of dumpsters, and panhandled for money every day. I had my little place in the bush that I called home. At nights when the sun would go down, I would come alive. In my mind, the darkness was my best friend. I would be your best friend today, and tonight rip you off blind, if I could. In this shadowed world of survival, there are no real friends and you cannot trust anyone.

People that work in these detox units, shelters, missions, and half way houses, live and work on the edge of the darkness of addiction. They become the doorway between the world of drugs and alcohol, and the enlightened world of sobriety and recovery. They are the lights shinning in a world of madness. Most of these people in this kind of work are survivors of the world of drugs and alcohol. Over the past fourteen plus years I have been in this field, I have seen twelve clients die from addiction. Not everybody that tries to reach recovery and sobriety will reach it. One of my clients was Stan. Stan drank until his liver was totally shot, and his heart had swollen to over twice its normal size. He had developed yellow jaundice and his body had swollen up so big he could not even move. Stan stayed this way for weeks, the doctors were able to bring him back, and they did save his life. The hospital released him after a couple of months, and told him that if he ever drank again he would be dead within weeks. Stan went right from the hospital to the liquor store, bought a fifth of whisky and drank the whole thing. Six months later, he was dead. Stan died at age thirty-five of multiple alcohol and drug related illnesses.

Another one of my clients was named Sharon. She had two children. The oldest child was eight. Sharon used heroin. Her way of taking it was with a needle, in the arm or leg. She soon came down with hepatitis C, but kept on using her drug of choice. Sharon continued using until she ended up being HIV positive. After years and years of heroin use by needle, her immune system was ruined. She gave HIV and Hepatitis C to several other people that had shared the needles with her. Sharon became very ill and not expected to live or get out of the hospital. It was many years in the coming but when she finally succumbed one week before her oldest daughter graduated from high school.

In 1996, I met a thirty-three year old man who had been drinking and using heroin for seventeen years. He spent the last twelve years of his life living in detox units, shelters, jails, hospitals, the bush, and in a mission when he could. I worked with this client for seven months. We arranged for his family to come out from back east to see him get his six-month chip for sobriety. They had not seen him for twelve years. They were proud that he was in recovery and came to see him get his chip. On the night after he received his six-month chip he got a motel room, shot up some heroin, overdosed, and died. He had written on a piece of paper, " just one more time". His family got this little note to take back east with them.

There are many more true stories like these I could go on and on with. Many of the people that live in these detox units and shelters where rejected by their families because of their addictions, and cannot go home. Many times, I have seen the pain in some of these people's faces. There I am on my way home and I can still see that look on those faces that shows they feel they will never go home. I know we will never save all these people, but I still get excited when I can see one of them turn their life around. Holidays are very hard on many of these people when it has been a long time since they last saw their children. I have seen some of these people crying late at night on Christmas Eve. They know they will have no Christmas with their family for the sixth or seventh year in a row. These people are just like anybody else that has never had a problem with addiction. They feel the same pains, have the same disappointments, and cry the same tears. I cannot emphasize enough the importance of good family ties to those in recovery.

Over the years, I have also seen many success stories, but one story stays in my mind. On one early October morning many years ago, I sent two men off from the East County Detox Center I sent them to a Menlo Park Inpatient Program for six months of intense treatment for their addiction problems. Each man carried all he owned in a plastic trash bag. I never saw these two men after that and just hoped the best for them. About three years after that rainy morning in October, I was working a graveyard shift at the East County Detox Center, 11 P.M. to 7 A.M. About two in the morning a real nice van pulled up to the detox parking lot. Two men, two women, and four children got out. At first, I thought, what is going on now?

They were starting to walk up the ramp to the door as I stepped out of the door. I asked them if there I could help them with something. One man looked at the other and stated, "He doesn't even remember us". Then one of the men asked me if I remembered that a few years ago I sent both of them off to Menlo Park around the end of October. I had to think hard because we sent people off to treatment all the time. Then they reminded me that I had told them both that nothing but good things would come from sobriety, and I suddenly remembered them both. They looked like two new people that had been rebuilt. They had gone on and completed their treatment. After reuniting with their wives and children, they obtained good jobs, and have stayed clean and sober ever since. They just thought they would all come and see me so they could say, "thank you very much". It was two weeks before Christmas. I felt like they had given me the greatest Christmas gift anyone could have ever expected to receive.

In Pittsburg, California, there are many rough gangs. One night at the East County Detox in Pittsburg, we had one of these rough local gang members in there. At two in the morning I went to shut off the TV in the lounging area and found this gang member was in the room. After I shut off the TV, I started picking up things in the room and doing a little cleaning. I went to the coffee table in front of this young man and told him to go get some sleep and I would take his dirty dishes to the kitchen. This young man looked at me with a puzzled look on his face and asked me, "Why would you do that for me". I stopped and sat down beside him and told him "Because somebody did it for me". For the next several days, this young man had a different attitude. He left the detox and went into treatment. After completing his treatment, he came and asked me to help him get away from the gangs. I call this a success story.

I was walking out of a shopping center, going towards my car, when I heard someone calling my name. Well, there were many people in this parking lot and I could not hone in on who was calling me right away. After I heard my name the second time, I saw this nice car. In the front seat, there was a young lady and a young man, and a child was in the back seat. As I walking over to the car, I had no idea who these people were. The young lady said, "Hi, do you remember me". I replied that I was not sure if I remembered her but that she looks like someone, I should know. She reminded me of her time in the S.S.A.C. Detox in Vallejo, CA. She recalled how I sat up with her all night trying to help her overcome her fears of sobriety. She informed me that she had gone into a long-term inpatient treatment program and completed it. She had gotten married, now has a daughter, and is now working for the county. She has stayed clean and sober and has a great life for herself. I always enjoy the chance to catch up with a client because their successes are my successes.

For every success story there are many more that are unsuccessful. Those are sad and depressing stories of people that did not make it one way or another. Some may have died while others may be in very bad medical condition. These deaths are not in vein, as long as we can remember them and use them to help inspire others to work harder to achieve their sobriety. I have a son that is seventeen years old now. When he was five or six years old, I took him around to all the detox units and shelters where I had been working. When I took him to the Shennum Center Detox there was an old man sitting outside the office. He was very dirty, had hair all over his face, and had a very bad case of the alcoholic shakes. He was a very sickly looking man that had lived a very hard life. I could see fear on my sons face when he looked at this old man. Looking back at my son and shaking very badly he stated, "Son, this is what alcohol and drugs will do to ya". Today my son is seventeen years old and he still remembers that incident as well as if it had happened yesterday. Now this old man is dead. Before he went to be with God, he made a lasting impact on a young boys life. My son has never touched alcohol or drugs. He has told many of his friends about this old man. This man has helped my son and many of his friends. He earned his place in the next life.

Working in the kind of work I do is not easy for most people. Many people have a home life that is always in turmoil and always seems to be falling apart. Many of these people go to work while hoping to be able to somehow fix their own home life. Most of these people end up fired because they have affairs with clients, relapse, or end up with major burnout. Anyone going to work in this field should first make sure their own personal life is in good order. You cannot help another person fix their life when your own is messed up. Over the years, I have decided to take a different approach to rehabilitation from addiction. I designed a program that starts right off with the birth of addiction. It starts with when the addictive lifestyle first got a foothold. Right away, I bring the whole family into the picture. Then the addicted person can start seeing how their addiction has affected there loved ones.

All the way through the ninety-day program anything associated with the person in treatment will be brought into the recovery process. All family, relatives, friends, work life, past, present and future. Some people may say the feelings of guilt for the mental and emotional pain the client has put everyone through is too hard on the client. I feel they should start knowing from day one of treatment the toll their chosen lifestyle has taken on the other people in their lives. Inside this book is a lot of information I use day to day in my recovery groups. I have designed all this information in order to broaden the area of recovery from just the one person to everything associated with them and their dysfunctional lifestyle. Over the years, I have had a lot of success with my approach to treatment. I have had a lot more success with my approach than I ever did with the standard methods of treatment. Many clients tell me that they are learning things in my recovery groups that they have never heard before.

THE TREATMENT BEGINS

DANGEROUS FEELINGS AND EMOTIONS IN EARLY RECOVERY

Eight different emotions and feelings that can lead to complications in early recovery are:

1. STRESS
2. DEPRESSION
3. FEAR
4. NERVOUSNESS
5. ANXIETY
6. LOST, OUT OF PLACE
7. LONELINESS
8. AGGRESSION

STRESS AND DEPRESSION

Feelings and emotions can be a major obstacle in early recovery. Early recovery is considered to be anytime during the first two years of your life of sobriety. Many things can bring on stress. One of the major causes of stress in early recovery is the feeling that there is too much expected of you right from the start. Many times the people in the AA and the NA groups tell the newcomers a whole lot of things they will have to do. Sometimes they will also use the threat of relapse as a tool to get them to do these things. Recovery should be simple leaving as much stress out of it as possible. Not something super hard and almost impossible. Another problem is the depression. Many times people in early recovery should seek mental health care for the problem of depression. They may or may not receive a prescription for depression. If they are put on an anti-depressant, it does not mean that they will be on anti-depressants for the rest of their lives. These prescriptions are an extremely valuable tool. The client should make the most of this tool during recovery in order to help achieve sobriety. Some individuals may need to take anti-depressants for only a while. The feeling that they may be unable to meet the high expectations of so many people during early recovery often adds to their depression. Depression can also happen when a person in early recovery expects too much of a change in their family members and friends. These changes do not always come right away. Early recovery is a time full of changes involving everyone concerned. Depression can also come when they feel alone if they never get involved in the AA and NA enjoyment activities. These enjoyment activities will help them become socially involved with others in their new life of sobriety.

FEAR AND NERVOUSNESS

There are about ten most common fears of recovery that will come later in this book. These fears are actually not real but they are very real to the individual who feels them. The most common fear is the fear of failure and the fear of how will I be able to face everyone if I fail. High expectations given to the client in early recovery by many well-meaning people at AA and NA meetings can cause the fear of failure. Some of these expectations usually come from sponsors. Especially if they are new sponsors or have very little experience. Most of the old timers know better than to put high expectations on others that are in early recovery. These fears in early recovery are a major cause of relapse. Nervousness is so common. At first we do not know how to act, or what to say to others, or what to do in public or around other people in recovery. At first, many people entering treatment get very nervous being around family and close friends. What do I say, how do I act, what will they think, is what is going through their minds. These people need to learn, and will learn how to just be themselves and act normal. Time is the best cure for this fear and nervousness.

ANXIETY/LOST, OUT OF PLACE

We naturally feel the uneasiness of being where we feel we do not belong. At first in early recovery we are in an environment, that we do not feel is right for us and this could cause anxiety. This soon passes as you grow in your early life of sobriety and recovery. The feeling of being lost and out of place for a while is very common. Most people in early recovery have no past life of sobriety to relate to. In a normal conversation, this is hard for people in early recovery. The only things they can talk about are their life of addiction, not their new life of sobriety. Many people that have never been in the life of drugs and alcohol do not want to hear this because they cannot relate to what you are saying at all. This is why it is so important to develop a good social life in early recovery. That way we can have other people to communicate with and associate with that will like hearing what we have to say.

LONELINESS/AGGRESSION

The basic rule in early recovery is no permanent relationships for the first two years of recovery. There is a very good reason for this. If we get involved in a relationship in early recovery, it most likely will be with a partner that is also in very early recovery. You start relying on each other for support instead of your sponsor and your support groups. Neither one of you are able to support yourselves, much less your partner. When one of you relapse there is about 90% chance that both of you will relapse. Neither of you are able to stand on your own yet.

Now we need to discuss people that are married and in early recovery. This is very tough because most of the time they are both afflicted with addiction. Most of the time there are also children involved. Later in this book, you will read a lot more on the family in recovery. In the situation where husband or boyfriend, and wife or girlfriend go into recovery, they will need to be under the care of an addiction rehabilitation specialist for months, maybe even a year or longer. Through counseling, both parents will learn that their most important thing in life now is not each other; it is their own recovery and sobriety. They will have to keep their weekly support systems totally separated and maybe go to a meeting once a month together. Many try going to all weekly meetings together but they both end up in major relapse. Both parents need to learn from the start that if one relapses, the other must go on for their own sake even if this means going on alone. "You will never be anything for anyone until you are first something for yourself." This is a fact that eventually everyone in recovery has to learn. I do recommend that any family in early recovery seek out the aid of a rehabilitation specialist.

AGGRESSION

Aggression is a major tool you use to survive during the many years of addiction. Many people start learning to use this tool during their early childhood. Usually from birth to twelve years of age if they were born into a family afflicted with addiction. When the person goes into early recovery, it is very hard to just stop using this tool. We do not know yet how to use all the tools of recovery. Every once in a while, we unwillingly use this old tool without even thinking about it. That is natural in early recovery. As time goes on in your new life of sobriety, this old tool of aggression seems to fade away as you start using the new tools of sobriety. If you find this does not fade away or you cannot seem to get rid of it, you may want to seek out anger management groups. These groups help you get rid of a menacing problem that will cause relapse. Any rehabilitation specialist can help in this situation. Ongoing counseling will help also. Overcoming aggression is a problem that is very common in situations where both parents are going into recovery at the same time. It can and does cause both parents to relapse because they do not know what they can do to get over this obstacle in their path to recovery.

THE PROCESS OF TREATMENT/THE ROAD TO SOBRIETY

When a person goes into treatment for addiction, we have a process must be followed. First you must go into a detoxification center for anywhere from five to thirty days. The length of the stay is determined largely by your attitude towards recovery. The drugs you are on, your age, your medical and mental condition are other factors. When you sit down with a rehabilitation specialist in a detox unit, they will be asking many personal questions. One of the first questions I ask a person at the intake is "*what are you willing to do to achieve recovery*". If the client asks me "what do I have to do", I know right away that there will be problems. This is the first sign that the client is putting terms on what they are going to be willing to do. The answer I am looking for is, "*I will do what ever I have got to do to achieve recovery*". I then lay out a verbal rough description of what the client can expect over the next seen days.

During the intake, I will be watching the client's body language closely. The first part of the intake I ask about their medical condition because the client may need to be taken or sent to a hospital for a medical clearance. This is done when a person has one or more life threatening medical conditions. The hospital may give the client some medications along with the medical clearance. Over the past years, there have been cases where the hospital kept the client and medically detoxed them. This happens when the medical condition is too critical to be detoxed in a normal detox unit. After you return with the medical clearance and maybe some new medications, the intake process continues. We take a completed history of your alcohol and drug use, family members' addiction problems, legal problems, and any history of treatment. We will go over the house rules and take you on a tour through the facilities. We make sure you are not hungry. You are given sleepwear and bathroom items. Then you are shown to your room. A bed awaits you there. We let you sleep for the first twenty-four to thirty-six hours, depending on your physical, medical and emotional condition. We watch you very closely while you are in the detox.

Now we want you to reach the point where you are stable and feeling a lot better. After the first, twenty four to thirty-six hours it is time to get involved in the normal detox activities. Some detox units have rehabilitation groups three times a day. All these facilities have an early morning chore list. Everyone is required to participate in these routine activities. Proper nutrition is an important tool in getting the client's physical health back. These detox units serve very good food. Soon you can eat normally. We are building up your health physically, mentally, emotionally, and spiritually. These detox units are set up to be as much like home as we can get them. There is a TV room, reading material, and lounging areas. The staff has an open door policy. This means anytime you want to talk, all you need to do is tell the staff. On your second or third day, we start right away working on getting you into a long-term inpatient or outpatient treatment program. If you are homeless, we start briefing you on possible housing programs in the local area. This will greatly assist you after the treatment program has been completed.

A detox program is also a pre-treatment program. This means they start getting you used to the intense daily, long-term treatment atmosphere of a long-term inpatient program. Inpatient means you will live there for several months while in treatment. Outpatient means you will live at home and attend treatment daily at a clinic. Some detox units have what we call extended stay beds. These are spots where a client could stay as an extension of the staff. This means you would help out around the detox unit with cooking, answering phones, extra cleanup, and other duties that may need to be done. These spots could be thirty day or ninety day slots. Most of the time, these slots are for people that may have a hard time getting into an inpatient treatment program. The staff is continually trying to keep your spirits up and keep you focused on your recovery. During this detox time there are many questions clients have and we try to answer them. You are taking what you may feel is a new step in your life and to you this may be all new.

When we were all born into this world the good Lord gave every one of us all the natural skills we would need to live a normal life, without the use of drugs and alcohol. Many of us were caught up in this darkened life of addiction to drugs and alcohol. We put all our natural skills on the back burner. Years later, after going into

Recovery, we think this is a new way to live. This thought could not be more wrong. In fact, when we go into detox and restart our lives without the use of drugs and alcohol, all we are doing is starting to learn to reuse these natural skills to live by that God gave us at birth. We soon find that this life is now new, but almost natural to us. We also start seeing the real "us", and what we were meant to be. We start liking this new "us" and this is when we start really growing in our life of sobriety. We also start finding that we have new interest in life.

Most people are on a natural high when that big day comes and they go into their long-term inpatient treatment program. By this time, they are feeling very good, their spirits are high, and they have started thinking about their future. A day or so before they leave for their program, the rehabilitation specialist may call them to the office to see if they have contacted their families and relatives. Many of these people have not had any contact with their families or relatives for many years. Many of these people do not want or are not sure if they should contact their families and relatives. This is not something we make them do. It is a choice only they can make. The counselor will be there with them to help them decide. If the client decides to contact their family, the counselor will try to make this happen. Many detox units will make the call so the client can reunite with them after being apart for however long. This is a big moment to these people. Reunion with the family clears one more obstacle in their paths to recovery. They find that they start getting the support of their families.

Many detox units will transport the client to the treatment program. Other detox units will help the client get the funds to get to the treatment program. When the client leaves the detox, they get strong support from the staff and other clients. When the client gets to their inpatient treatment program, they find a very warm welcome from the staff and clients. They start feeling as if they are a part of something big. They start getting their pride, dignity, and self esteem back. This is not a new pride, dignity, and self esteem at all. This is the positive pride, dignity, and self esteem that they were given to develop at birth. The clients are writing letters to their families, attending intense rehabilitation groups, and learning the major tools they will need to maintain a life of sobriety. They will develop a new bunch of friends that are not lighting up a joint. There will be friends that will be talking about their future in recovery. A good inpatient treatment program could last anywhere from sixty days to one year, depending on the type of program. Most people that go into treatment are under weight because of the years of abuse and not eating well at all. They find themselves gaining weight and feeling as if they can almost do anything.

As treatment comes to an end preparation begins for their departure and entry into their after care program. Some inpatient treatment programs have their own annex, or after care program, called transitional housing. It has an after care program set up for you. You could be in this transitional housing for ninety days to one year. You are allowed to come and go. There is a curfew in most of these houses set for no later than 11 P.M., unless you work nights. You are also required to attend the outpatient treatment programs attached to these transitional housing programs. Transitional housing is to help you process back into society and live a normal life. There are times when someone in transitional housing relapses. When this happens, the client is sent back into inpatient treatment for a refresher course and then sent back to transitional housing. Some people do need extra treatment to get to the point they are trying to reach.

When the client has completed the transitional housing, he is ready to go back to living a normal life. They will be set up with by-weekly one-on-one counseling for the next thirty to sixty days. By this time, they have been attending AA or NA weekly support groups. They have a sponsor and have been calling the sponsor every week. The rehabilitation specialist will help the client reach the point where they will no longer need to meet with them. That is when the client will begin using their sponsor only. The whole treatment process goes from day one at the detox to the end of the transitional housing. It could last from twelve to fourteen months, maybe longer, depending on the treatment program.

WHAT HAPPENS AFTER TREATMENT

When a person goes into early recovery, they start using AA and NA meetings for support after their treatment is over. Many times when you step into AA and NA meetings for the first time you may feel verbally bombarded by other people also in early recovery. You start hearing how hard it is. Most of these people have only a few months or maybe a year in recovery. Many of those people will start telling you what you will have to do to keep clean and sober. Everyone has a different opinion and everyone thinks they are right. God bless these people because they are trying to help by sharing their most personal experiences. Many years ago, my sponsor started me out on the right foot. My first two weeks in AA meetings I experienced this same thing and it scared the hell out of me. My sponsor told me to ignore all of that and do not worry about reading the big book and doing the twelve steps right now. He started me out with just learning how to get up in the morning, going to work, getting home clean and sober, and doing the same thing tomorrow. I worked for about fourteen months on this and got it down.

After I was sure I could keep doing the same thing from day to day, I did buy a big book. I started reading it on my own and the sponsor helped me with the twelve steps. I was doing this because I wanted to, not because I was scared into doing it. I was able to comprehend it and get everything out of it. My sponsor made it so easy for me that I could see from the start that I could do this. My sponsor's idea on early recovery was that if you could get to where you can live from day to day and keep clean and sober, this would be sixty percent of the battle. You would have the rest of your life to get the rest of it down. He was very right about this. By doing this the way we did, I was able to also learn to enjoy my life of recovery as I was learning how to live it. I learned many little things that helped me in my very early, vulnerable life of sobriety.

There are two parts to a good weekly support system. There is the serous part, the AA and NA meetings, outpatient treatment, one-on-one counseling, and a few other things. Then we have the fun part. Like going to the coffee shop with a bunch of guys after the meeting, pot luck dinners, clean and sober dances, AA camping trips and much more. There are other things like going out to eat or to a movie with some clean and sober friends. The fun part is what helps us to learn how to enjoy our life of sobriety. Without it, we are on a one-way road to relapse. So many people in AA and NA groups never get into the fun part at all. They will end up in relapse or living on a dry drunk. A dry drunk is a person that must be in recovery but they do not want to be in recovery. You will see two types of people in the AA and NA meetings. You will see some that are always laughing and seem to be having a lot of fun and joy out of being there. These people are the ones that have developed the enjoyment part of their support system. You will also see the ones that always look mad, grumpy, or in a bad mood. These people might attend seven or more meetings each week. I would not question their recovery at all. These people may have five, ten, or more years of recovery. They have never developed their lives of fun and enjoyment in their life of recovery.

The biggest obstacle a person has to deal with in early recovery is to learn to live from day to day and not drink or use. This is not a job you are taking on this is a lifestyle you are trying to develop. The first years of sobriety and recovery you are going to deal with all the physical changes that happen when changing from a life of addiction to a life of sobriety. The second year of recovery you will deal with the emotional changes that happen when changing from a life of addiction to a life of sobriety. The third year it all starts coming together and mellowing out. After that, you start developing a lifestyle. This weekly support and staying clean and sober start to become a natural part of everyday life. Doing the twelve steps and reading the big book is not what in going to keep clean and sober. It did help me a whole lot to understand the life of sobriety. I will still attend a meeting after fifteen years of sobriety. If you do learn how to live a good life of sobriety, keep clean and sober, and enjoy your life of sobriety you are doing fine. Even if you never are done with the big book or the twelve steps you are doing fine. You will have the rest of your life to do the twelve steps.

If you are trying to develop your life of sobriety by somebody else's schedule or set of rules you stand a strong chance of developing resentment and going into relapse. There is no set of rules or schedules to this. The strongest sobriety is the one that comes slowly and at the individuals pace. Set five times aside a week that you

are going to use to attend a support system like AA for the first two years. Set three hours aside each week to learn and study.

Call your sponsor every Friday night. The reason you should call you sponsor every Friday night is because if you get used to calling them all the times when you don't need them, when you do need them you will call. If you never call your sponsor, you will never call them when you are in trouble. As I stated earlier, when we were all born into this world we all received all the natural skills we would need to live a normal life without the use of any drugs or alcohol. When the addictive dysfunctional lifestyle took a hold of us these natural skills where all shoved in the closet. Many years later when we give up drugs and alcohol and live a life of sobriety all we start doing is using all the natural skills we received at birth. This is all new to us at first because we have had these natural skills but we have never used them. We start seeing who we really are and we start liking the person we are seeing.

CHAPTER 2

The family of the addicted family member has a much harder time in treatment and recovery than the addicted person does. Their recovery is much more mental than physical. Their recovery takes a lot longer to start showing positive results than the recovery of the addicted family member. There are major trust issues to deal with. Major financial problems brought on over many years of abuse. The family suffers from all the outstanding legal issues brought on by the addicted family member. Under proper professional care, the family unit has a very strong possibility of becoming a family again.

THE FAMILY GOES TO TREATMENT ALSO

BY W. LEE

BIRTH OF ADDICTION

ABOUT 70 % OF MOST OF THE PEOPLE THAT ARE IN BONDAGE TO ADDICTION WERE BORN INTO A DYSFUNCTIONAL, ADDICTIVE FAMILY UNIT. DURING THEIR PUBERTY STAGES OF LIFE THEY WERE TAUGHT ALL THE TOOL BY THEIR PARENTS THEY WILL NEED TO MAINTAIN THE SAME DYSFUNCTIONAL ADDICTIVE LIFESTYLE AS THEY BECOME ADULTS.

ALCOHOL & DRUGS USE ALL THE TIME
POLICE CALLS TO HOME
CPS WORKER INVOLVEMENT
POOR MEDICAL CARE
VERY LITTLE FOOD
ALWAYS DIRTY CLOTHING
POOR SCHOOL GRADES
LEGAL PROBLEM FOR FAMILY
NEVER MUCH MONEY FOR FAMILY
CONSTANT FIGHTING
POLICE ARE THE BAD GUYS
ANGER & VIOLENCE RESOLVES PROBLEMS

WHAT ELSE CAN THIS CHILD LEARN DURING IT'S PUBERTY STAGE OF LIFE IN THIS FAMILY UNIT THAT IS IN BONDAGE OF ADDICTION.

PARENTS

FAMILY UNIT

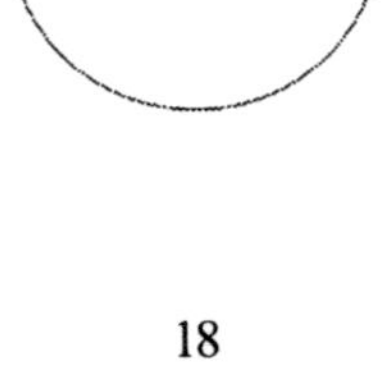

ARE THE PARENTS AT FAULT?

WERE DID THIS DYSFUNCTIONAL LIFE OF ADDICTION BEGAN?

WHAT ARE SOME PROBLEMS THIS CHILD WILL FACE AS THEY GROW TOWARDS ADULTHOOD?

When a father or mother goes into treatment for addiction the spouse and children, also go into treatment. If a rehabilitation specialist is assigned to the family from the start, they will start working with the family members from day one. The family members are also the victims of addiction. Sometimes their treatment is much harder than it is for the adult with the addiction problems. In the family, you have the codependent, family hero, scapegoat, mascot, and lost child. These are the roles found in the dysfunctional family unit. The codependent is also known as the enabler. This is the one family member that unwillingly, but totally, supports the addicted member of the family, which is normally the father or mother. The family hero at about twelve or thirteen will also take on the role of a parent-child.

ROLES IN THE DYSFUNCTIONAL FAMILY UNIT

Over the years, I have always been told there are four types of dysfunctional family systems. I have found this to be very true. I also feel that alcohol and drug use is involved in all four types of dysfunctional family systems.

1. The Alcoholic and Drug Dependent Family System
2. The Emotionally Disturbed Family System
3. The Physically or Sexually Abusing Family System
4. The Religious Fundamentalist or Harsh and Unpleasant Family System

The relationships within the dysfunctional family unit are very unnatural but to the family members it is normal. This is because one of the family members has problems that affect the whole family unit. This will force the other family members to adapt family roles that will focus all their attention on the family member with the problem in order for the family to survive as a unit. The family members problem is usually addiction to alcohol and drugs. This is usually one of the parents, either father or mother. Their total daily focus in this family unit is to keep this addiction going for the addicted parent.

CODEPENDENT OR ENABLER

Most of the time, these roles are found in the family unit that has a problem with drugs and alcohol. The spouse in these families may enable the partner with the addiction by lying for them to their employer. Codependency or enabling becomes a major problem for the spouse that does not have the addiction problems. The codependent spouse's role or daily duties become focused on caring for and enabling the addicted partner. The children also assume roles in the dysfunctional family unit that will focus on supporting the addicted parent.

The codependent will protect and care for the spouse with the addiction, in order to keep the addicted spouse from having to deal with the consequences of their addictive, dysfunctional lifestyle. The codependent, or enabler, will feel angry and resentful, because their whole life is centered on caring for the spouse with the addiction. By the codependent's efforts to keep the addicted partner from feeling the consequences of their actions, the codependent is condemning the family to staying in the dysfunctional situation they been living in.

THE HERO

The hero is characteristically over-responsible and an over-achiever. The hero may excel in school, be a leader on the football team, or maybe a cheerleader. They are usually suffering from painful feelings of inadequacy, and or guilt, because they cannot fix the family's pain. The hero's compulsive drive to succeed may in turn lead to stress-related illness. The hero feels isolated, unable to express their true feelings or to experience intimate relationships. They are often out of touch with their own sources of spirituality.

They get praise for their achievements from family and friends. What they are really trying to do is fix their families pain.

HERO IS OFTEN THE PARENTIFIED CHILD

The family hero tries to gain recognition and approval and tries to be independent. They will feel guilt, fear, anger, loneliness, and confusion. The other role the hero will play is that of the parentified child. This is because the hero is the oldest child. The hero will take on his role of the parentified child as they go into adolescence, and sometimes before that. The parentified child is the child that grows up through early childhood to the age of twelve or thirteen, and is forced to give up their teenage years which is known as adolescence. Because both parents are wasted and drunk most of the time the oldest child, the hero, will be the main caregiver to the younger children, this is the role of parentified child. The parentified child sees all their friends doing things that teenagers get to do and yet they are left behind because of their adult duties. The parentified child will do the cleaning; cooking, getting the younger children up and ready for school, making sure the other children get their homework done. The parentified child will take on the adult duties so their younger brothers or sisters will be able to play and be children.

The parentified child will have a lot of anger, rebelliousness, and resentment. They are known to run away at a very young age. The anger and resentment keeps building within the child and when other children take advantage of them and make fun of them in school, this adds to the pain and pressure building up in them. One of the biggest problems about parentified children is that when they cannot be children when they are children, it comes back on them later when they are adults. Later in life, they will act out their childhood that they were deprived of during their childhood. This could cost them jobs, or relationships, or the ability to progress in life. It can also affect their ability to maintain recovery from addiction. It will affect them mentally also. There is help for this problem but it is a long process just like being in recovery from addiction.

THE SCAPEGOAT

The scapegoat most of the time is the second oldest child. They are known to act out, show anger, and are usually very defensive. Even though they will act like a delinquent. They feel a lot of inward pain and resentment because the dependent person and hero always get all the main attention in the family, and they feel ignored. The scapegoat is very likely to be the first to use drugs and alcohol. They will always get very poor grades in school. They may become sexually active at a young age. They will start hanging out with gangs and getting in trouble with the law. The hostility, attitude and anger of the scapegoat may bring them to the point of violence to others, bad accidents, major injuries, and prison. This could make the scapegoat the big family problem. Now they are starting to get all the attention instead of the family member with the addiction. What the scapegoat is really saying is "please help me." When the family starts to see the need and tries to come to the aid of the scapegoat, this can lead the whole family into treatment and recovery. The scapegoat plays a big part in getting the family into treatment in many cases. The scapegoat may develop leadership skills among the gangs they hang with, but these leadership skills are all very negative.

THE LOST CHILD

The lost child feels like they are not a part of the family unit. They will feel distant, and become withdrawn, isolate off to themselves, and feel lonely. They are very shy children and develop their own little world of fantasy to retreat to. The lost child has poor communication skills, problems in developing good relationships, and problems sexually. They will use sickness, bed-wetting, disobedience and rebellion to gain attention. They will find comfort in several pets, or get deeply involved in church feeling these things will solve their problems. The negative attempts to escape might be what lead them to avoid seeking professional help, and so many will remain hidden in their isolated world. Most of the time, the lost child has few friendships, and has difficulty finding a lasting marriage partner.

THE MASCOT

The Mascot's role is clowning around most of the time. The Mascot will have a lot of fear and anxiety and could grow to adulthood still acting like the child. Many times the mascot is overprotected from problems of everyday life. The Mascot is often the youngest child, trying to be the center of attention in the dysfunctional family unit. The mascot will try to entertain the other family members to help ease the pain. Instead of dealing with problems, the Mascot will run away from them. If this inner anxiety, depression, and desperation are not debt with by professionals, it could cause the child to go deeper into mental illness. Later on, the mascot could become dependent on drugs and alcohol, and this could lead to suicide. The Mascot has problems with friends because they often will be criticized, rejected, and made fun of in school. There is a big probability that they will develop learning problems in school. When they are the only children in the dysfunctional family unit, the child could take on all four family roles, depending on the situation within the family unit at the time. This could cause the single child to have all the problems of all four roles in the dysfunctional unit.

The children will have a different set of areas to deal with when the family goes into recovery along with the addicted parent. Their issues may be **rejection, mental abuse, physical abuse, major depression, fear, extreme anger, violence, trust issues, malnutrition, poor medical condition** and others. As you can see there is a lot more to it than just quitting the drugs and alcohol. That is just a little part of the rehabilitation of the dysfunctional family unit. It is good to get the whole family working with a rehabilitation specialist so the specialist can get the appropriate services involved to help all the family members. The treatment for the women and children is much more intense. Their treatment is a lot longer than it is for a father going into treatment for his addiction. Children are so fragile and venerable in early treatment. It may take children weeks or even months to get to the point were they feel safe enough to open up to a child therapist. Young female children may have hidden issues of rape sexual assault that they do not want to talk about at all.

In treatment of a whole family in early recovery, there are many professionals involved. There are **medical exams, mental health therapists, women specialists, rape crisis counselors, child specialists, addiction rehabilitation specialists, family therapists, BWA, AA, NA**, and a few others. All these services are set up by the point person that starts the process with the family. This is normally the rehabilitation specialist. All these services will work together for the success of one family. It takes a while to get all these services in motion. Meanwhile the most important ones in the dysfunctional family unit are also the most vulnerable. These are the children in the dysfunctional family unit. A rehabilitation specialist will start right off trying to give aid and support to the children. There may be other issues with the family unit, like **stable housing, on-going case management, or clothing for the children for school**, and many more issues. Many dysfunctional families are living in their cars, or with friends, or relatives when they go into recovery. Most of these families have very bad credit histories and it may be very hard to get housing for these families. There are housing agencies in almost every city to aid these families.

In the past, rehabilitation counselors would not deal with the whole family because they did not have the skills to do this. They would only work with the family member that was afflicted with the addiction. This always left the rest of the family out in left field to deal with their problems themselves. This caused major family problems when the husband or wife would come home after months of intense treatment. They would come home expecting the whole family to meet them with smiles, and open arms. This was not happening at all. Instead, the family members would be withdrawn and untrusting. They did not know how to be supportive of the returning family member at all. This would cause resentments with the returning father or mother. They would still be expecting this total trust, respect, happy and smiling, welcoming family. With treatment and counseling the other family members will learn how to be supportive of the returning family member in recovery.

CHILDREN OF THE ADDICTED FAMILY UNIT ENTERING RECOVERY

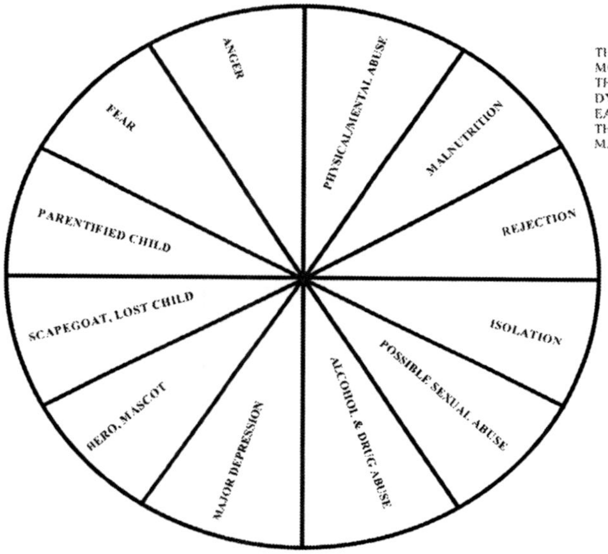

THE CHILDREN HAVE SEVERAL MORE AREAS TO DEAL WITH IN THE DRUG & ALCOHOL ADDICTED DYSFUNCTIONAL FAMILY UNIT IN EARLY RECOVERY THAN THE FATHER. THIS ILLUSTRATES THEIR MANY AREAS.

These family roles often go right into adulthood. Throughout childhood, the children are learning what it will be like for them for the rest of their lives. When they play out these family roles in these dysfunctional family units, these roles become a permanent part of their lives. They cause major problems in their adulthood. These children develop marriage problems, relationship problems, cannot keep jobs, addiction problems, and they end up teaching these roles to their children.

MINIMIZING, PROJECTION, INTELLECTUALIZING & DENIAL

Tools used in codependency

MINIMIZING is to know there are problems but believing it to be really nothing at all.

PROJECTION, is putting all the blame for the problem onto others.

INTELLECTUALIZING, is making a good excuse will make the problem go away.

DENIAL is refusing to believe there really is a problem.

These are the major tools used with the dysfunctional family unit. It could be a major family problem but by acting as if it is nothing at all, minimizing, it never gets resolved. No matter what the family problem, it is easy to put the blame, projection, off onto somebody else, maybe another family member. By making an excuse for every family problem, intellectualizing, will make the problem just go away. Believing there never was a problem, denial, makes everything just fine and rosy. There is very poor communication in the dysfunctional family unit. These children grow up not being able to trust anyone at all. They are unable to make good decisions because they do not trust their own ability to make decisions. The dysfunctional family members are often closed off from the rest of the world.

Some of the rules the family members live by in the dysfunctional family units are:

1. They can't talk about any problems,
2. They can not express feelings or honesty,
3. Communicate indirectly, through acting out or another family member,
4. You can not have any fun,
5. There is no talking about sex,
6. Never challenge your parent's actions or anything they say,
7. Don't model after your parents, [do as I say, not as I do],

There are several other rules to live by in these families depending on the severity of the dysfunctionalism in the family unit. Living by these rules makes it very hard on the children in school and other public events. They start having mixed feeling because they see other children that do not have to live by the same rules they do. As these children get older, this starts causing major problems within the family unit because the children rebel.

MOTHER/WOMEN IN EARLY RECOVERY

In the dysfunctional family unit, it is harder for the women or mothers going into treatment than the father. There are twelve areas of this dysfunctional lifestyle for the women to deal with. This does not mean that every woman will have all twelve areas to deal with. Each of these twelve areas can be broken down to expose many other issues. Along with the threat of **continued alcohol and drug abuse,** they have the physical and mental abuse that goes along with the domestic violence in many dysfunctional family units. **Mental abuse** turns women into almost a state of slavery in the family unit. Every thing she does is focused on trying to keep an addicted, abusive, angry husband or boyfriend happy so he will not get angry. They go without all the time in order to provide for the children as much as possible. Many of these women find a way out of this abusive situation when they get into recovery and find themselves alone with two or three children to provide for. They are right away, faced with **affordable housing, getting an income, and having food to eat**. Most of these women that get out will start on welfare and other government services. Many of them get training and end up getting jobs and bettering their lifestyles.

These women have major problems with **communication and relationship skills**. I am not saying they cannot communicate. I am saying that when they are left to start dealing with life on their own, they seem lost at first. They may feel fear when they are applying for a job or being interviewed by a man. Leaving a long time abusive husband will often be the cause of these problems, they will face at first on their own. If there is a knock on the door, they may not answer the door in fear that it may be their ex-husband or ex-boyfriend. If they get a job, they may have a very hard time dealing with men in a business environment. Many years later when they decide to try dating they may find they just cannot trust any man. When these women first find themselves alone and caring for their three children, they find themselves needing **money management services.** They may have some **old traffic tickets or other legal problems to deal with**. They might have an **old DUI** from their past. These women often find they have many skeletons in the closet.

Many women survivors of a dysfunctional, abusive relationship find they **have no job skills. They will have to go to school for job training.** They might have to take daily living skills classes. It is not uncommon for them to end up having to deal with **CPS to get their children back**. It seems like CPS does more harm than they do good. Some women go to a rehabilitation specialist to get help in dealing with CPS. One of the hardest things for CPS to deal with in a court is to face a rehabilitation specialist. I have been up against CPS three times in support of my women clients getting their children back and won all three times. Most of the time women that break away from an abusive relationship have been unable to see a doctor or get medical care for themselves. They have always cared for the children first and there was never enough money to use on them. When they get on their own, they need **medical and many times mental health care for a long time**.

Some of these skeletons in the closet they end up dealing with is **rape**. This is the hardest issue of all and the one they will hold until the last. Most of the time, these women were raised from birth in an abusive, dysfunctional family unit. To many of these women, using drugs and alcohol was meant as a medication to help them deal with the abuse. Over years of drug and alcohol abuse, it became a major addiction. These women are very vulnerable to more abuse. Without good help and treatment they will go right back into the same type of relationship. These women are very strong codependents and this increases their vulnerability. These women will start having children very early in life and by the time many of them are twenty-one years old they already have two or three children. This puts a major burden on their chances of getting an education and being able to get good jobs and take care of themselves and their children. Most of these women were victims from birth.

When many of these women have to deal with CPS, they are required to a**ttend family therapy and parenting classes for months**. They are required to attend **group therapy many times,** along with **addiction rehabilitation groups, BWA groups, and AA meetings**. On top of this, they are being both mom and dad to the children. They now need to make a living, act like there is nothing wrong and smile all the time. The treatment for addiction is a few months of intense treatment. **The treatment for all the years of physical, mental, and sexual abuse will go on for many years to come**. Some of the many problems these women are faced with are **fear, aggression, anger, major depression, constant stress, nervousness, and suicidal thoughts.** When you have a person in constant turmoil, trying to deal with all these emotions going on all the time, you have a major problem. They will most likely start living on their own free from their abusive partner at or below the poverty level. To some of these women this is a big step down but to be free from the abuse is worth it. In times like these family members can both be a major help and cause more problems at the same time. At times family members are ready to tell the woman what she should do, when she should do it, and how she should do it. The best thing family members could do is listening and give strong support.

Their ability to function normally in society is distorted. However, with intense treatment and care, this too will pass and they will become productive in society. **Through one on one counseling, group therapy, family classes, BWA groups, addiction rehabilitation groups, and a loving family,** their lives do get better. This seems like a lot but this is what it takes to deal with the abuse and the addiction. This is not including the other ten areas they will be dealing with. The survivors of battered relationships become a very powerful support to those new members of BWA as they come in.

WOMEN/MOTHER/CODEPENDENT IN EARLY RECOVERY

WOMEN OR MOTHERS HAVE SEVERAL OTHER AREAS TO DEAL WITH WHEN THE FAMILY GOES INTO EARLY RECOVERY. IT IS DIFFERENT WITH EACH PERSON. SOME HAVE MORE AREAS THAN THIS AND THEY WILL NEED MORE CARE & TREATMENT.

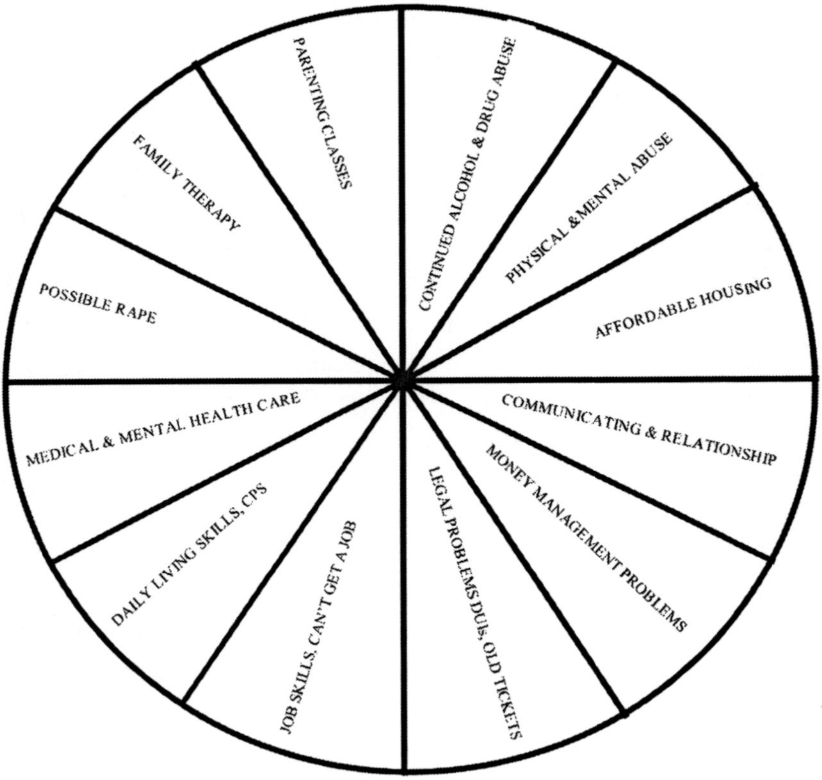

SURVIVAL SKILLS TAUGHT DURING CHILDHOOD

The birth of addiction is when the addictive lifestyle to alcohol and drugs was first introduced into your life. It is not when you first started using. Most people in bondage of addiction were born into a family unit where alcohol and drugs were used all the time. Childhood is from birth to 12 years of age. In a normal family unit, the children grow up learning life skills. In the dysfunctional family unit afflicted with alcohol and drugs the children grow up from birth to 12 years of age learning survival skills they will need to survive in the darkened life of addiction. The real hell is when they start putting into practice these survival tools.

These children grow up to twelve years of age learning to be very cold hearted, and never learn to identify with their own true feelings. The only law they will learn to obey when they get older will be the law of the streets. They will learn to live in the shadows of existence, the darkened side of life. There is still hope for these children. It may come during their adolescence, in time to save them from some hell on this earth. As to the survival skills these children must learn, they will learn that anger and violence will get you what you want. Another skill they learn is how to use drugs and alcohol. Often they will learn this through their parents or friends. They will learn when to talk, whom they can talk to, and what they are allowed to say.

These children are taught early in life that all police are the enemies. The children are taught that they are not to talk to police. Never tell them anything about what really goes on with family or friends. This is hard to believe but it is the truth. In these dysfunctional family units, it is common for CPS to be involved in their lives all the time. These children are taught that all CPS workers are not to be trusted and never tell them anything at all. They learn that hunger is an everyday part of life and that they have to just deal with it. Because of the cost of drugs and alcohol, there is never enough money for food for the family unit. They also learn that constant depression and stress is normal in life. All they have ever seen in their young lives is a constant state of stress or depression so this becomes a normal way of life to them.

Stealing is an acceptable means to get what you need and want, and is learned very young in life. There are people that teach young kids how to steal in stores. They have no concerns about the hardship stealing could put on someone else. They graduate to where they are stealing lawnmowers, bikes, cars, and then wind up in jail. It is not long at all, until these young kids learn they do not have to try in school because nobody cares anyway. Most of the time, their report cards are not even looked at. They learn how to skip classes and hang out with the bad crowds. They do not have to do what the teacher tells them because there are no consequences anyway. They learn that in life as they know it there are the "them and us", the "them", are the police, the system, teachers, and anybody else that is against the family. The "us" would be their family unit or their street friends.

In these dysfunctional family units, they learn very fast that drugs and alcohol always comes first. They come before food, clothing, medical needs and any other items that the family members may need. After the drug and alcohol needs are met, the family may get what is left. The bills might be paid. The kids might get lunch money for school. It is ok not to respect any other people and to use bad language towards them. It is ok to refer to women as "bitches" and to call men "bastards" because mom and dad do. To these children growing up in these dysfunctional family units "love" is just a word; it is nothing to be felt. One of the worst things they learn early in life in these dysfunctional, addicted family units is that anger and violence is what you use to control other people. Next, we will get into what happens when these kids reach adolescence and start putting into practice the survival skills they learn during childhood.

REACHING ADOLESCENCE

The children that grew up in these dysfunctional family units from birth learn their negative survival skills and by the time they have reached adolescence, they naturally start trying to perfect these negative life skills. They will feel drawn to the bad crowds because they feel like they belong there. They will start leaning other negative life skills from their peers in these bad crowds and they will teach some their own skills to others. These kids start identifying themselves as gang members. This soon becomes their

LIFE/SURVIVAL SKILLS TAUGHT IN THE DYSFUNCTIONAL FAMILY UNIT TO CHILDREN FROM BIRTH TO 12 YEARS OF AGE.

During our childhood [from birth to 12 years of age] the child will learn many survival skills. During these year the child will have only 2 main teachers in life, their parents. This does not mean their parents are wrong at all. The parents will teach only what they have been taught in life. To the child, their parents are never wrong no matter what.

Anger & violence will get you what you want
How to use drugs & alcohol
That all police are our enemies
CPS workers are against us and are not to be trusted
They learn that hunger is an everyday part of life
Depression is a normal
Its ok to steal
You do not have to try in school, because nobody cares
The "Them & Us" attitude
Alcohol & drugs come before food, clothing, medical care, and anything else.
Its ok not to respect other people
Love is just a word
Violence and anger is what you use to control other people

new family and they start feeling a very negative kind of love from the other gang members. To these kids, bad love is better than no love at all. They will develop an all-new bond that becomes a closer bond than they ever felt at home. In the new street family of theirs the use of drugs and alcohol is an everyday part of life.

Violence, fighting all the time, gang violence with rival gangs becomes a big part of their new everyday life in these street gangs.

Death becomes an acceptable part of this life they are living. Their natural families start becoming a distant part of their past. As a gang, they steel anything they can that will bring in money. Dealing in drugs becomes another everyday job for them. They soon graduate to steeling cars, breaking into homes, robbing fast food stores, anything to support their gang and the gang habits. Going to school to get an education has all but stopped. They have been kicked out of school so many times they just stop going at all. The only world they know is their gang world. This world will have a disastrous end for them all if they choose to stay in this world.

Trying to develop relationships with friends becomes a major problem for these kids. They can only relate to other kids just like themselves so they have nothing positive to offer to anyone in a relationship. Sexually related diseases run rampant with these kids. Some are AIDS, Hepatitis A, B, C, D, & E and several other diseases. It is common to find some of them with terminal drug related and sexually related diseases by the time they are sixteen years old. The kids that end up with terminal diseases before they are even old enough to vote find it hard to look forward to any kind of normal adulthood. It will be almost impossible to have a mate and a normal relationship. They will end up with a very early death.

Most all of these kids will have a record with the law before they reach sweet sixteen. Many of these children will have been in and out of jail many times before they reach their eighteenth birthday. Some of these kids will become eighteen while in prison. Prison is no place for a teenager, because they are quickly being snatched up by the older inmates and many are used as women. These children stay away from home, sometimes for days. They may check in at times to see what is going on at the old home place. Their other family members quit trying to control them. Many families do not want them around anymore. Most of these kids are victims of drugs and alcohol and get addicted very fast. This is when their world really starts falling apart. There are many children in special treatment programs just for kids getting treatment for their addiction to alcohol and drugs.

When many of these children see many of the other kids they were in school with doing very well and going places in life depression starts setting in. Some think suicidal thoughts because their lives have been a living hell and they cannot understand why. They do not know that they did not even have a fighting chance from the start. They do not understand that the lifestyle their parents chose to live programmed them for a life of the same exact thing. The more depression sets in, the better suicide looks as a means of escape. A lot of these children will never see their twenty first birthday as a free person because they will end up in prison early in life. They are charging children as adults now in many states. Some of these kids will see prison from sixteen years old to thirty years old, missing the most important parts of their lives. There are ways to stop this and get these children the help they need early. Thereby giving them the fighting chance, they deserve to have in life.

ADOLESCENCE, YEARS OF HELL

Once children reach 12 or 13 years of age they are ready to test their life skills they have been learning from mom & dad. As I stated earlier, in the addictive dysfunctional family unit, these skills are all very negative and will cause major negative repercussions for them later during their teenage years. Right at the start they find themselves being drawn towards other kids that are like them that have come from the same type of family environment they came from. As these kids start hanging together, they will start using their negative survival skills at the expense of anyone that is vulnerable. They will also gain knowledge that is more negative and devastating from these newfound friends. Soon these kids perfect these negative survival skills. These kids find themselves members of a local gang. Now they are hanging with the wrong kids because they feel a since of belonging to something.

The negative lifestyle these kids have started with will soon lead to using drugs and alcohol. These habits will cost money, so soon they are lead to steeling small things to support these habits. Soon these kids find themselves in street or gang fights and many are being hurt or killed. The minor steeling soon turns into major steeling of larger things like "cars". They have been steeling money from family members for a long time. They may even steel grandmothers SSI check because they know they can get at least 30% of it's value on the streets. Their gang becomes their new street family and they do feel some kind of love. Even if it is a very negative love, at least it is something. These kids have been kicked out of regular school so their continued education will be from the dark world of drug and alcohol. The only real relationships they can develop are with others just like them, so these relationships are all negative also.

By now, these kids are staying out very late at night. Often they do not even come home for many days. Their family members do not even know if they are alive or dead. Their main daily activities focus on the streets and their gangs. Their focus is not on their real families anymore. Most of these kids end up addicted to drugs and alcohol before they are 18 years old and are in need of major help. As I stated earlier, many of these kids end up positive with Hepatitis "C" or positive with the HIV virus before they are 18 years old. They will not even know this because they do not go to doctors anyway. They will be passing this Hepatitis "C" or the HIV virus around to others for many years before they even know they have it. Once they find they are infected with one or more of the incurable diseases, they feel their whole life is over.

Many of these kids will never see a wedding day. They may end up being killed because of the lifestyle they have had to live. Some of these kids start seeing death as their final future. This can be brought on for by many reasons, maybe by seeing their lives are going down hill and they do not know what to do to stop it. They see other kids they went to school with doing very good and starting good lives for themselves. They start wondering why they have to live like this. Many of these kids have serious crimes pending against them. They know that if they are caught, they will end up in prison for a long time. Some of the kids that know they are positive for Hepatitis "C" or positive with the HIV virus, feeling they will be dead before they are 30 anyway so what is so wrong with suicide. They feel they will never be able to have a life anyway so why keep on living. They start feeling so very alone and feel like they have nobody anymore, nothing to live for, and nothing to loose.

This all started when they were born into the dysfunctional family unit and was taught all the negative survival skills of life instead of the positive life skills that would have aided them in going the right way in life and having a good life. Now, is it entirely all mom & dad's fault? No, mom & dad just taught the only things they knew, because this lifestyle is passed down from generation to generation, long before mom & dad. There are many resources to help dysfunctional families to get back on the right track in life and keep their children from having to live the life mom & dad had to live. We need to fight with everything we have to save the children and keep them from going into these teenage years of hell.

DEFINING THE LIFE OF ALCOHOL AND DRUG ADDICTION

The best way to give a definition describing a lifestyle of addiction to drugs and alcohol is to make a list of everything you can think of bad that could happen to you and your family and you will be very close. Addiction to drugs and alcohol will affect everybody you will meet in only a negative way. Anyone and everyone you know and associate with are used to maintain your addiction. To the addicted person everyone is a tool used for his or her survival.

Adolescence, the years of hell

During adolescence the child use all his/her survival skills as normal living skills. During these years the child will become well known by the police, their own relatives will reject them because they do not want them around. They will seek out and find an alternate family [street gangs] that will teach them another kind of love. This is the life these children are distend to live.

They will learn other survival skills from his peers
They will start perfecting these dysfunctional life/survival skills
Hang with the wrong crowds because they feel they belong there
Drinking & using drugs
Fighting all the time
Steeling money and other valuables
Kicked out of school a lot
Major problems developing relationships
In trouble with the law "them & us"
Staying out late at nights, running the streets
Addicted to drugs and alcohol
Could start having suicidal thought
Headed for prison for steeling cars

The only thing that is ever positive about an addiction to alcohol and drugs is when you go into recovery from your addiction. When you think about this, how could any of us expect the children that had nothing but negative experiences for the first nineteen years of their lives to be anyway near normal? For every negative action in life, a negative reaction comes back to you.

DEFINING THE LIFE OF ALCOHOL AND DRUG ADDICTION IN THE DYSFUNCTIONAL FAMILY UNIT

DOMESTIC VIOLENCE

1. Spousal abuse
2. Child abuse
3. Elderly abuse
4. Sexual abuse

POVERTY

1. Very little food for children
2. Dirty clothing

3. Utilities shut off all the time
4. Gang involvement
5. Prostitution
6. Deceases [sexual & drug related]
7. Shattered family units
8. Poor education
9. Poor medical care
10. Poor employment skills
11. Poor living conditions
12. Homelessness
13. Death on the streets

LEGAL PROBLEMS

1. Shoplifting
2. Dealing drugs
3. Steeling from family members and friends
4. Warrants
5. DUI's
6. Steeling cars
7. Assault charges
8. Murder
9. Armed robbery
10. Sexual assault [rape]

THE DESPERATE CHILD

Below is a chart that illustrates the spiraling, down hill life that most all children borne into these dysfunctional family unit will be forced to live. In most cases, the parents have no idea at all of what kind of life their child will be living because they are blinded by their own addiction to drugs and alcohol. I am sure that if they only knew, they would take steps to stop or avoid this terrible lifestyle their child will be forced to live. Addiction blinds a person to the realities of life as well as the hell their addiction will take their families through. There will be nothing positive at all these children will have to look forward to in life. Many time we hear about a child being arrested for murder and the parents getting on

TV saying how good their child was and how well he was raised. By saying this, they can avoid feeling any blame themselves. I have always felt that the parents should be looked at as well as the child that committed the crime. There is nothing wrong with the courts making the parents go through a year or two of parenting classes. This might help to stop some of these crimes that these children commit before they are real serious.

Controlling these children might be out of the question for the parents by themselves. Many of these children by now might be staying out late at nights or maybe even for days at a time. Many young girls end up as mothers before they are even adults. They end up alone, homeless, and with child. Soon they brake off all contact with family and relatives, because after they have become pregnant their families point the finger at them blaming them for their situation. Many times the families and relatives totally reject the child and will not let them even come around. The majority of these children find they are addicted to multiple drugs and alcohol. Society looks at these children as another bad apple on the streets. The big question is who is responsible for this situation these children are in. It cannot be the child. Even if the law looks at them as young adults, they are still children because they never had a chance to be a child. The blame lies on the shoulders of the parents, the courts, and society itself. When the legal system starts seeing a child heading down the wrong way in life, that should step in at that point and get the family the professional help that can stop this before it reached the point that their child is charges with a serious crime as an adult. If there were an intervention ordered by the court on just 30% of these dysfunctional family units that are devastated with addiction, this would keep a major percentage of these children off the streets and out of jail. The families that would get the help they need would be able to stay together and grow together.

The children that are caught up in this spiraling, down hill path in life would make several attempts to turn their lives around but these attempts will be in vain. These attempts would be tried later in their teenage years. The reason why they will not a successful on their own is that they were never taught normal, positive living skills during their childhood. You cannot take negative survival skills and make them work positive. If there is no help offered for these children, they will end up in prison, on drugs, or dead. Society should look into the faces of these unfortunate children and they would see a look that would scare the hell out of them. These unfortunate children all have that far away look that tells you they just do not care anymore. Relatives can step in, help their relatives in need, and stop the loss of so many children. In my line of work we see this far away look in these young kids faces all the time and you want to just take the pain away from them and somehow make everything ok for them but you know you cannot fix everything.

THE DESPERATE CHILD

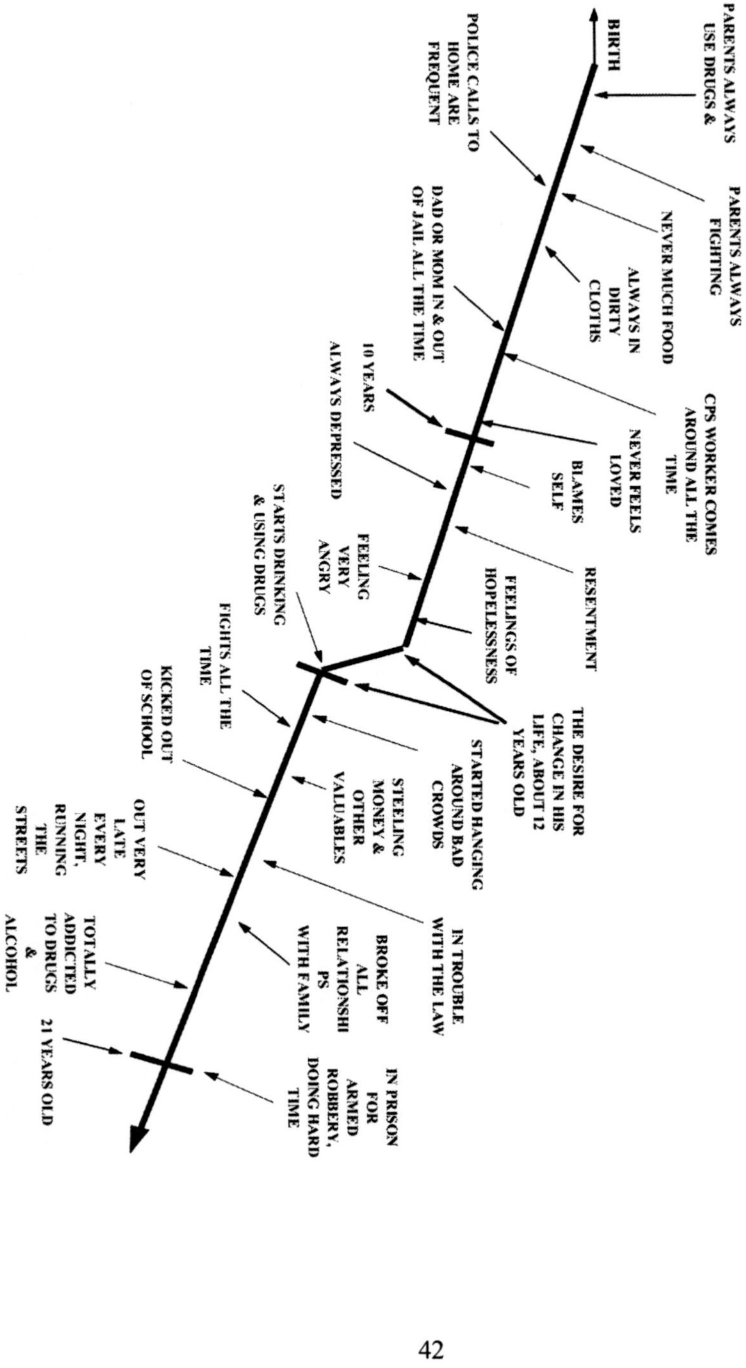

CHAPTER 3

THE THREE LEVELS OF ADDICTION/THE LONG ROAD HOME

LEVEL ONE

We grow into our first level of addiction. It can start with stopping for a cold one after work a couple of times a week. Even though we do not know it, many of us start a gradual escalation in our drinking and or drug use. Before we know what is going on we have gone from a one time a week stop at the bar to seven times. We have gone from just a couple of beers to being drunk when we leave. This time span could have been a few months or many years to get to this point. All this time we have been managing to hang on to our job but our credibility at work has become threatened. It is not long before we start putting something other than coffee in out thermoses when we go to work. This will help us to maintain ourselves at work hopefully, without being detected. We are very good at keeping this from the boss but it is not long until some or our friends see through us and see what is going on. This could go on for years. Remember, there are only two ways out of a life of addiction to drugs and alcohol, one is a good life of recovery and the second is death by addiction.

The biggest problem we run into is the few people we work with that are in recovery from addiction. These people can see through us like a plate glass window. They have already been there, done that, and got caught. Some of the close friends we work with have come up to us and attempted to talk to us about what is going on. We right away reject them because they just do not know what they are talking about. There seems to be a war going on within us because we have to keep our high going and look normal at the same time. This is just like taking on a second job that we are not being paid for. We used to sit around with the other guys during lunch brake and coffee brakes but no more. Now we sit by ourselves and isolate because we do not want any of them to know what is really going on. We try to smile when we want to frown, and laugh when we want to cry.

By now we are well into our addiction to alcohol and most likely some drugs also. We still look at ourselves as being normal, or as if nothing is wrong at all. We cannot see the big change in us over the years of our alcohol and drug use because it has all come on at a very slow rate of growth. Soon our personal life seems to be in turmoil, we have tried to keep the bottles and the drugs hidden so the rest of the family does not see anything. We think they do not know but we are just fooling ourselves. They have all known for a long time. Some of the bills have been going unpaid and we are not keeping the grass mowed anymore. We have not been doing anything with the children on the weekends for a long time and the spouse has become a distant person in our lives. Our personal appearance has gone to hell and we do not seem to care much about it. We still think everything is normal. When anybody tries to tell us different we reject what he or she have to say.

Gradually it gets to where our biggest concern is maintaining our addiction and nothing else matters. In many cases the physical abuse starts. Many men have forced their wives to go into the Battered Women's Program. Physical abuse and addiction go together hand in hand. This abuse is to the wife, the mother, the girlfriend, the sister, dad, brother, and anybody else that is close to the addiction person.

Does this person afflicted with addiction know what is going on? The answer is "yes", and at the time, they do not care. In the mind of the addicted person any and everything becomes expendable in order to maintain their addiction. The family members start becoming distant people to us and they do not want to have much to do with us anymore. This has not caused the family to lose any love for this addicted person. The family goes into the self-preservation mode and the person afflicted with addiction starts becoming expendable. These feelings set-in because the family members do not know what else to do and the preservation of the family takes precedence.

As the body starts breaking down we find it getting much harder to maintain that mellow high and function in society and the work place without anybody knowing just what is really going on in our life. We find we cannot just stay mellow. We are either wasted or sick and the ability to just maintain is gone. Once we have reached this point in the addiction we can never get back. The good old times of just maintaining our high and still functioning normally in society will never again be a luxury for us to enjoy. Our sick time has run out at work and we are loosing more and more time on the job. The morning drink or joint to mellow us out does not work anymore. We have to have four drinks or three joints now. This takes us well over the top and going to work is not going to happen. There is no food in the house and the savings account is at zero. What cash the family has left is going to go for more drugs and alcohol. If it is the husband afflicted with addiction, the wife starts trying to negotiate with the husband to get some money for food for the children. Speaking of the children where are they by now? The children seem to have gone into hiding by this time because of fear of being abused. This does not work because the addicted person seeks out the children and their abuse continues.

The addicted person has been using anger and violence as a means of maintaining total control over his or her family and environment. This is done in order to keep all money and valuables going to maintain their addiction. Everybody around them and his or her money and valuables become expendable. The wife or husband, of the addicted person tries desperately to hold the family together. This leads to becoming co-dependant to the addicted one in a desperate effort to maintain some kind of peace in the family. In many cases, the co-dependant also gets into using drugs and alcohol to cover up the pain of the abuse. This leads them right into their addiction. The medical and dental care for the children has not been maintained for a long time. With the power cut off, no food in the house, the rent unpaid, and the phone cut off that addicted persons number one priority is still to maintain their addiction at all cost.

By this time, the wife of the addicted husband gets desperate and starts reaching out to any friends, family or anybody else that might be able to help her. Her nerves are shot. Even with the physical and mental abuse, she starts thinking about her priority, the children. Her number one concern now has changed from maintaining the family unit to rescuing the children. For years, she has been telling the children, "Daddy is just sick". This has not worked for a long time. The children know what is going on. Through all of this, the family love for each other is just as strong as it has ever been. The wife's thoughts are mixed between holding the family together and the need to salvage what she can of the family unit. All the advice from the relatives to leave him is starting to make some since to her. She is starting to look at this as a possible solution. In her eyes, she is feeling very helpless. Her own possible drug and alcohol use is getting to be a problem. There are two types of addictions. There is the direct addiction, which is the person afflicted with addiction, and the indirect addiction, which is the person in the bondage of the addicted person. The indirect addicted people are the ones that suffer the most from the addicted person. These are most always the family members of the addicted person. As to what was indicated earlier, the main goal of the addicted person is to maintain control over everybody and to keep all resources going towards maintaining their own addiction.

LEVEL ONE
DENIAL & ANGER

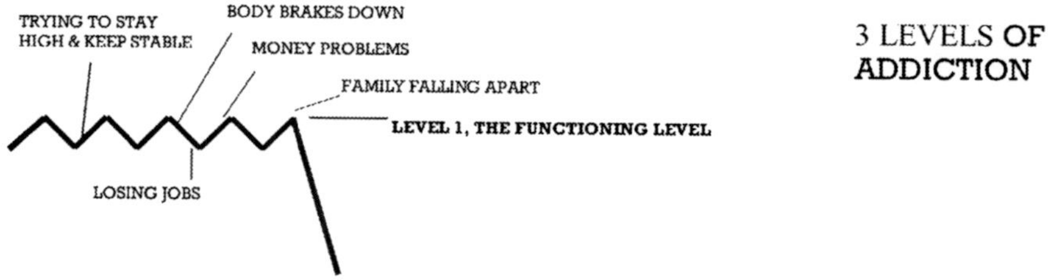

LEVEL TWO, THE COLLAPSING LEVEL

Level two, is the most destructive level. The addicted person's denial is now stronger than ever. In their eyes, they have never done anything wrong at all. Whatever has happened is going to be somebody else's fault, at least in their mind. The addicted person's anger has reached the point where no body can really communicate with them, other than a professional Rehabilitation Specialist that trained in this field. His self-esteem, pride, and dignity have been lost. At this point some people start thinking, "Why should I keep on living". They feel like everyone's out to get him or her and they think they have not done anything wrong at all. While dad is gone to get some more alcohol or drugs, mom has taken the children and left. He returns home to find an empty house. In most cases there is not even a note left telling him where they have gone, just that they have left. She has most likely gone to be with relatives. Then these relatives become supportive and protective of her and the children. The reality of what has just happened sets in and anger begins to rage through him. There is a since of relief now because he can really live it up and do whatever he wants. He may even start feeling a since of freedom.

The destruction of the family unit has happened. In addition, the only main concern of the addicted husband is still to get his drugs and alcohol. By now the addiction has escalated to the point where almost of value has been sold to support the addiction. With the wife and children gone and the husband evicted from the house he starts a life of homelessness. He still has a few friends he could stay with that are still sensitive to him and his situation. Over the past few weeks, his life has been going down hill as if he was on greased roller skates. The person is running from the law over a DUI he got a month ago. The job has been long gone, the car impounded, and soon these few friends will reject him because they don't want him to be living with them and abusing them. The love this family has is still as strong as it has ever been. It is just distorted by the power of this addiction. This once strong family unit with a stable future has been reduced to ruble. Often suicide starts looking like a good way out.

There will be a completely new set of rules to live and survive on by now, this person will learn these rules the hard way, and it will be costly. His deep down love for his family is still just as strong as it has ever been. The power of addiction takes over every physical and emotional part of the persons being. It is almost a supernatural force overcoming a person's will. The person may forsake everything in their lives that has any meaning to them at all. The person afflicted with the power of addiction is in bondage to this force. In this level a man's anger and denial has become the foundation for his life of addiction. The anger and denial is the very power that supports and keeps the addiction active. He does try to contact his family occasionally telling them how he is going to get help. This continued promise soon is ignored by the family. Again, this man falls even deeper to the final level of addiction. The first level on addiction goes on for years but the second level could just be a matter on months. At the beginning of the second level, the person is watching TV, eating at his own table, smoking dope, and drinking booze. A few months later, he is sleeping in a box in the bush, eating out of dumpsters, panhandling and hanging out at the local liquor store. He has not changed clothing for a long time and there is a very strong odor around him. The power of his anger and denial has also caused him to reject society and all their efforts to help him. The person has now reached a level in society that most people do not want to deal with at all. He has now reached a point in life to where he is on the outside looking in. He is thinking of what he once was and what he is now.

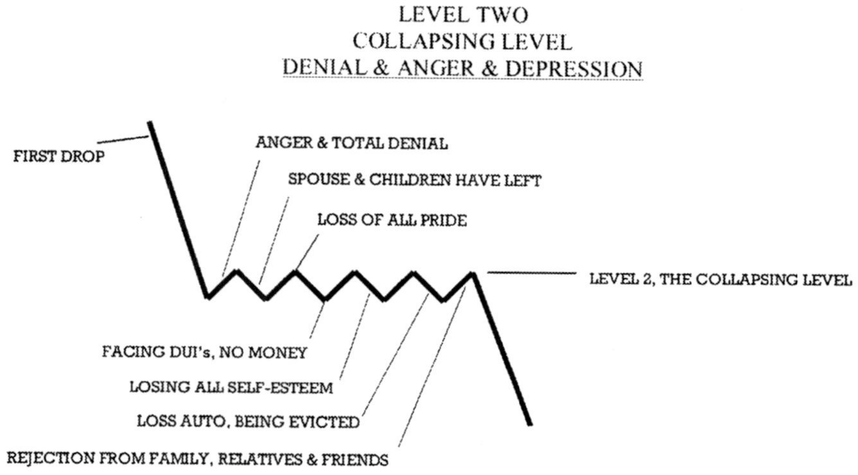

LEVEL THREE, JUST SURVIVING LEVEL

At this point in the person's addiction, they have started adapting to this new lifestyle and have been learning the tools of survival needed to live this lifestyle. This man has a new place to live, it is called a cubbyhole, or in the bush. He also has a new place to eat, it is out of a dumpster, or in the soup line. He has another job at his favorite panhandling spot. The pay is not good but it will due for now. His favorite thing to do now is to hang out at nights on the streets with the guys. The nights are cold but he has learned to adapt to this. His relatives, family, and so-called old friends will not have much to do with him anymore. This could go on for years like this. He has not seen his wife and children for a long time. He has long since quit calling them, not even occasionally. He still dreams of how his life was at one time. There have been many thoughts of suicide as a possible way out. By now, this does not seem so very bad. His face is bruised from fighting in the streets. This person's medical condition is now much worst and he is starting to feel it. His ankles are starting to swell up and there has been a yellow look in the whites of his eyes. This is related to major liver trouble.

There are still has some old legal issues he has been running from that are all related to his addiction and maybe child support issues as well. He has gone from the good life with a family to living in the dark side of life that most people do not want to recognize the existence of. Perhaps he is suffering from cirrhosis of the liver, hepatitis A, B, C, D, OR E, yellow jaundice, or enlarged heart. There are many illnesses related to addiction to alcohol and drugs. His short-term memory seems to be failing him a lot now. His mental condition has gotten so bad that he does not have the ability to think clearly or reason normally anymore. It has reached the point where nobody wants him around at all anymore. Even the police do not want to take him in. He feels like he does not have anywhere to go, turn, or run to now. He reaches the time in his life that everyone afflicted with addiction meets eventually. This I call the final "Y". At this time, he will make the final decision to get help, go into recovery, or experience death from addiction. If he chooses to go into recovery and get help, his mental and medical condition will start getting better. The other path will bring death very soon.

LEVEL THREE
DEPRESSION, & ACCEPTANCES

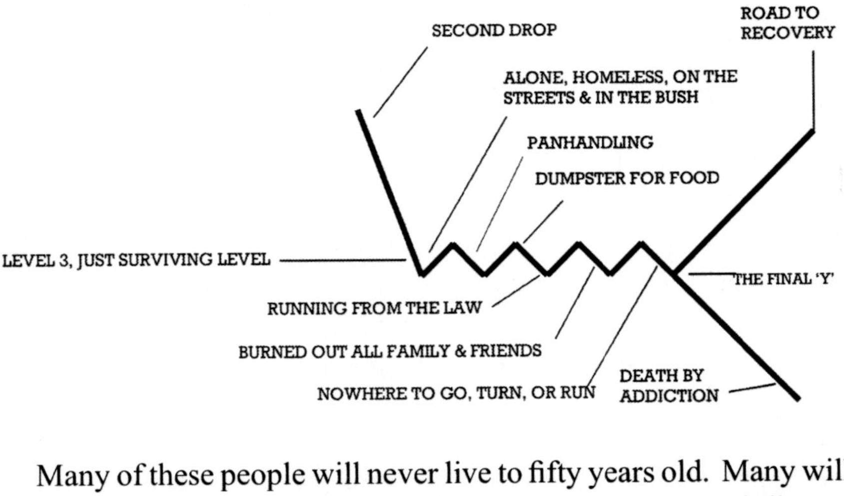

Many of these people will never live to fifty years old. Many will die by the hand of the law, many will die of fatal venereal disease they acquired during their adolescence, and many will die by their own hand.

THE COMPLETE THREE LEVELS

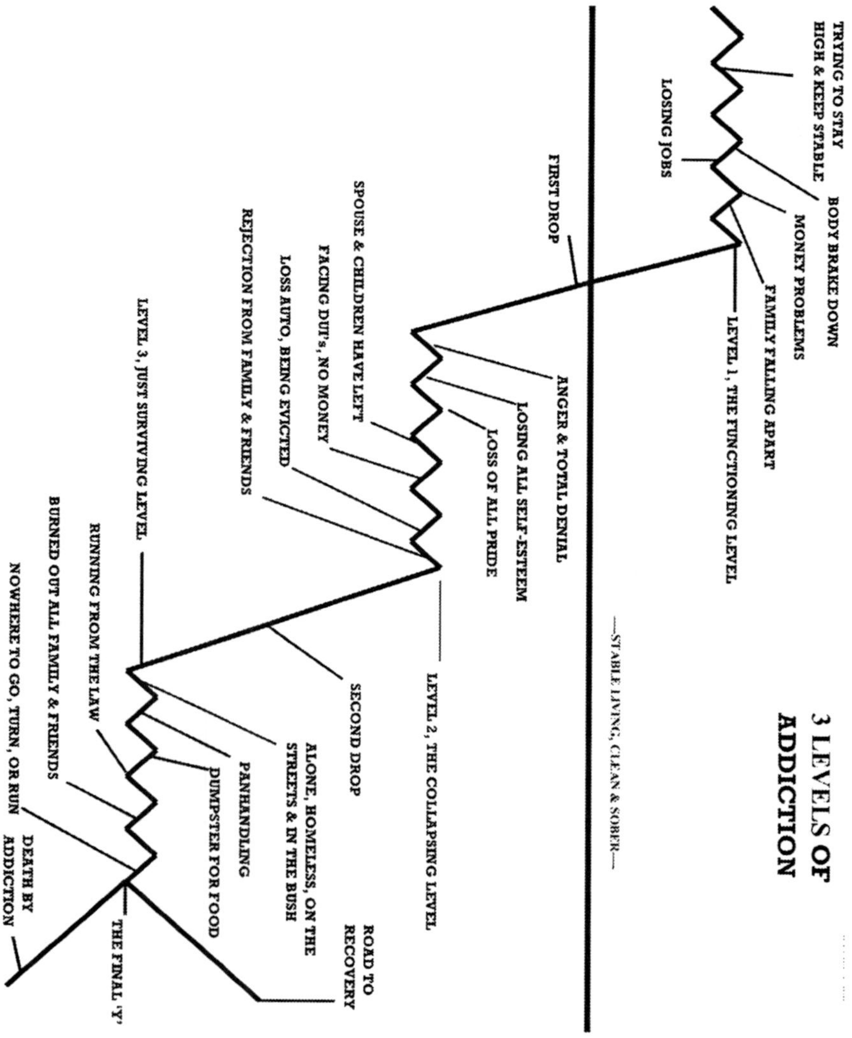

THE LONG ROAD HOME

Once a person has reached the end of the line and has made the final decision that they are giving up this life of addiction they start the long road home. It took many years to get were they are in their addiction and it will take a long time to get to the point where they will have some strength in their recovery. This long road starts with a good detoxification unit for anywhere from 5 to 15 days depending on what they are detoxing from. During this time, the person will be around other people that have been through what they are going through. These people will help him along his way towards recovery. Detox Specialists know how to deal with the normal problems that the person will be facing during their stay. After about 3 or 4 days when he is feeling much better they will help get in touch with many of the inpatient and outpatient treatment programs that the person will need to help him learn to live a life of sobriety. There are things that a detox specialist needs to be on the look out for during this detoxing time that could be dangerous to the person detoxing. The specialist is trained to spot these possible problems and they know how to act accordingly.

The most dangerous thing that needs to be watched for is the seizures that often come when some people are detoxing. These are known as alcoholic seizures because they are triggered by the heavy withdrawal from alcohol. If a person is over 40 years old and has a history of heart trouble these seizures can cause a heart attach and death. Another of the problems that can cause death very easy is a person who is detoxing from Heroin and Methadone at the same time. This puts too much of a strain on the heart and other parts of the body if they do not get immediate medical treatment. Another major problem is depression that comes with detoxing from alcohol and drugs. Many people end up having to get medication for this depression. They have been high on alcohol and drugs for so many years and they never knew they had a problem with depression. They also find that they have to start facing the realities of life that have been covered up by their active addiction for so many years.

Many times the fact that their families have long since rejected them is one of these just realized realities, adding to the depression.

Some of the other realities are the old legal issues that will have to be cleared up so they can get a new start. This process starts right at the detox unit itself. The detox specialist will start preparing them mentally to face these issues in life. The rebuilding of the client's self esteem is also started right away during detoxing. The detox Specialist is the person that will begin the recovery process. They have been trained and they are very good at their jobs. Once the person leaves the detox and goes into long-term inpatient treatment this takes them to another level of life. They are with many other people that are set on doing the same thing with their lives. This inpatient treatment program should be no less than 90 days long. Anything over 90 days is better, the longer the program, the better chance the person has of making a good life for themselves. While they are in this impatient treatment program, they will learn the many tools of recovery they will need to live a life of sobriety.

These people are given the best of foods, good medical care, and expert guidance. They will learn the reasons why they must attend a support system for the rest of their lives. They will also learn to understand their family members when they seem negative towards them. Inpatient treatment programs are very intense and they have several group sessions all day, every day. These people start becoming bonded to the others they are in treatment with. This almost develops into a family unit and they soon learn things about each other that end up helping all of them. Once they are getting close to, the end of their impatient treatment the counselor will start setting up their aftercare and preparing them to face a life of sobriety. This brings on some uneasy feeling that is normal. Most all programs will have a follow-up outpatient treatment for their clients that will last from 6 months to a year after they have completed their program. This follow-up outpatient program is to give them continued intense support as they face life in recovery. Living a life of sobriety is not a job it's a lifestyle.

During the first year of sobriety, the client will go through the physical changes from a life of addiction to a life of sobriety. During the second year of sobriety, they will go through the emotional and mental changes from a life of addiction to a life of sobriety.

During the third year, this all comes together as one and it starts turning into a lifestyle. This process cannot be hurried or speeded up. It must go at the pace that is good for the client and every client has a different pace. In recovery, a year is still 12 month but the individual's progress may be longer than a year. What one client achieves in a year another client may take eighteen months to achieve. Most people go into recovery with nothing more than their clothing and maybe a few belongings. Usually most these people have lost everything they had to addiction. Recovery or sobriety starts the rebuilding of their whole life.

Many of the people that go through an impatient treatment program end up relapsing within a few weeks or months after they have completed the program. This is expected because we know that not everybody is going to make it the first time. It is very hard for a person to go back to the program and say they blew it, and have to do this all over again. This is why many of them do not come back easily. It gets a little depressing for the client at times when they run home to show their families their one-year chip and their families just look at it and say "that's nice". This negative attitude from the family is only a built in safety switch they have developed. They do not feel years of addiction and hell from this addicted family member is going to go away that easily. When one family member goes into recovery the whole family unit goes into recovery. The family unit's recovery will take just as long as the addicted person's recovery takes or longer. In my own life, my wife and I have been together for 18 years. I have been in recovery for 16 years. Many times, she still thinks of what would happen if I start drinking and using drugs again even after 16 years. I have no problems with this fear that she still has because it is also a part of her recovery. Responsibly is another very hard thing for a person new in recovery or sobriety because they have gone many years avoiding any commitments. Many of these people have to get help in learning how to even pay their monthly bills. Many of them have a hard time keeping a job because it is the first job they have had in many, many years.

Attending a life long support system is necessary for anybody in sobriety. The best support plan for the first two years is to set five times a week aside that you will be going to meetings Do not let anything or anybody get in the way of these five weekly meetings. After two years, you can drop this to four times a week for the third year. At four years, you can set this to three times a week and keep it at that for several years. There are two parts to a weekly support plan. The first part is the serious part, the 12-step meeting, the learning how to live in sobriety, and all the other tools you will need. The second part is the fun part. Going to the coffee shop after the meeting with friends, clean and sober dances, AA or NA camping trips, going out to eat and to a movie with clean and sober friends, all this and any other activities that can be done in recover helps to develop this into a lifestyle. The fun part is just as important as the serious part. In many cases the fun part is needed more that the serious part.

THE LONG ROAD HOME

THE LONG ROAD HOME

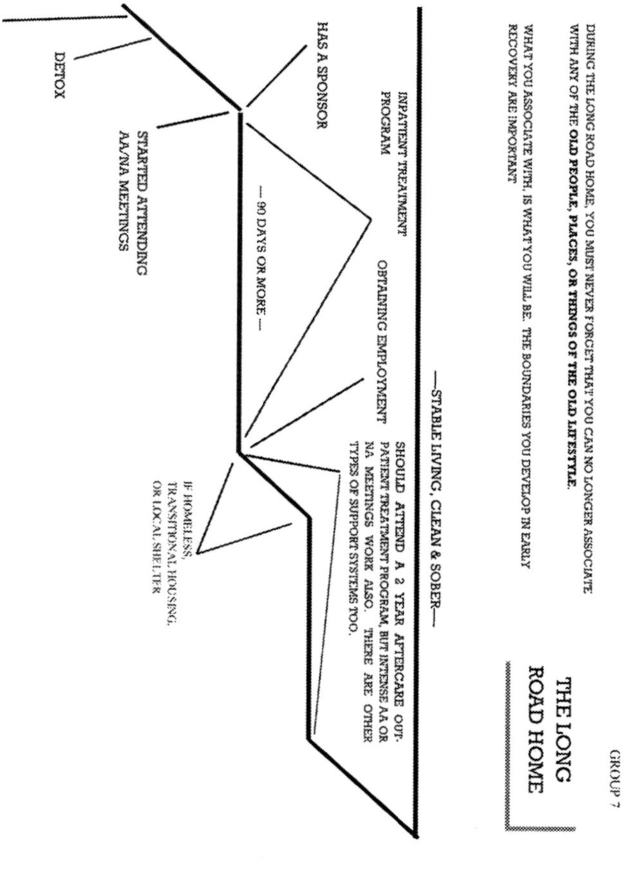

EIGHT MAJOR AREAS OF THE DYSFUNCTIONAL LIFESTYLE OF ADDICTION FOR MEN IN EARLY RECOVERY

Continued Alcohol and Drug Addiction is the backbone, the main force, that will keep the addicted person spiraling to the point to where they will reach death by addiction. Denial is the main force that will keep the addiction alive. His addiction will go on until his internal organs will not be able to function anymore and death comes. His addiction causes the whole family to face a distructive force that will distory their unity. Affordable Housing, is a major problem for them because all the money they have will go to support his active addiction. This also causes the whole family to suffer. The addicted father has very little reguard for what he is putting his family through. Relationships and Communication Problems are problems because the only people he can relate to and really communicate with are other people with drug and alcohol addiction, just like him. He/she finds it very difficult to carry on any normal conversation unless drugs and alcohol are involved. They will never be able to maintain a job because of this problem. They will never be able to deal with everyday life's problems because of their active addiction. When he/she goes into early recovery they will need help from professional counselors in dealing with these problems.

Financial Problems, Can't Handle Money, will be a problem in early recovery because the only places he/she has ever had to deal with was when making liqure store purchases or making a transaction with a drug dealer. A good daily living skills class will fix this poroblem and get them on the right track. Very soon his family will start feeling the positiveness reflecting from his developing good financial skills. Legal Problems, DUI Charger, Past Unpaid Tickets, can be a major problem for at least 50% of people that enter early recovery. There is a process to prep the client when going to court to deal with these problems. A certificate showing he has completed detox. A long term inpatient treatment program with a twelve month outpatient after care program makes a big inpact on the judge. He seems to get real light on the fines and penalties. No Job Skills, Lack of Training, is an on-going problem with people in early recovery. After the treatment is over it is good for a person to get the best job they can and start taking night classes towards getting certified in a field of work that will pay them a good living wage for them and his family. It is not real hard to start taking just one class each semester towads this goal. As time goes on you can increase this to two classes per-semester. Soon you will be done and a whole new world will open up for you.

Anger and Violance Issues, are very common with men in early recovery because these were the main tools of survival during their lives of addictrion and living in that darkened world. When they go into early recovery these issues are not real easy to get rid of. Sometimes ongoing counseling, one on one help, and maybe even anger management classes are needed to help overcome this problem. For several months after recovery has started little outbursts of anger may occur but this is short lived as he learns new living skills. Medical and Mental Health Needs are areas of their lives that have gone without care, for years in many cases. It is always good to get started in their medical needs right away. This is a very big part of their recovery process. Sometimes some of these eight areas of the dysfunctional life of addiction will open up other areas that will need to be addressed.

THE EIGHT MAJOR AREAS OF THE DYSFUNCTIONAL LIFESTYLE OF ADDICTION THAT MEN GO THROUGH WHEN THEY ENTER EARLY RECOVERY FROM ADDICTION.

ADDICTION

THE EIGHT MAJOR AREAS OF THE DYSFUNCTIONAL LIFESTYLE OF ADDICTION THAT MEN GO THROUGH WHEN THEN ENTER EARLY RECOVERY FROM ADDICTION.

THE DYSFUNCTIONAL LIFESTYLE OF ADDICTION

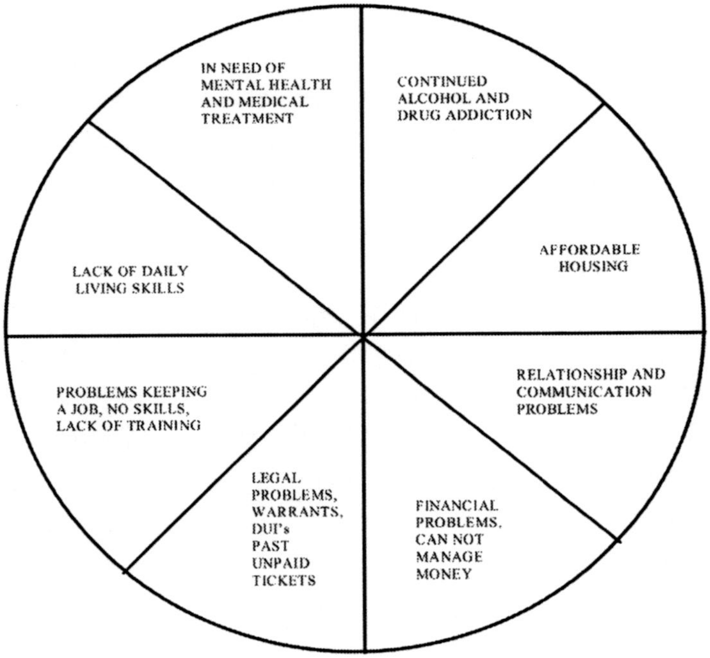

CHAPTER 4

FROM ADDICTION TO RECOVERY

LIFE OF ADDICTION

The life of addiction brings the person down to the level of life that is a living hell. A person could live with a chronic addiction for five years, to twenty years, to a lifetime. This lifestyle takes you to the lowest level of existence. Every thought and action is totally focused on maintaining your addiction. This road leads to being homeless, joblessness, mental breakdown, health problems, broken families, legal problems, loss of all pride and self-esteem, and much more. It could lead to suicide.

FEARS OF RECOVERY

There are ten most common fears of recovery from addiction. There is fear of success, failure, change, reality, obligation, responsibility, fear of yourself, facing family members, legal problems, fear of acceptance and rejection. Most of these fears are not real but they are very real to that person. These fears need to be addressed one at a time. Most of the time, when a person makes it past the first fear the rest of the fears seem to be easier to deal with. The best form of treatment is to start with the fear that would be the easiest one to deal with. These fears are major obstacles to a person's early recovery.

THE CHARACTERISTICS OF A CLEAN & SOBER LIFESTYLE

What a clean and sober lifestyle means is that you are being responsible, well focused on yourself and where you want to go, and that you are dealing with the skeletons in the closet. It also means you are maintaining a good weekly support system. You must always keep an open mind and be empathetic towards others. One of the big problems with a life of addiction is that we never finish what we start. Now we must start learning to complete anything we start. We must learn to develop good daily living skills. People, places, and things from the old days are the biggest cause of relapse. One of the most important things we must do is to develop all new people, places, and things that are positive. Boundaries are very important. You must have strong, positive boundaries in your life of recovery. Red flags are our built in warning signals that tell us we are on dangerous ground. When we start seeing these red flags we need to take notice very fast. The family members are the last people to have any faith in us. We must have patience with the family members and let them have their time they need for recovery. Even when we are having a very bad day we can try to keep thinking positive.

TOOLS FOR EARLY RECOVERY

Early recovery normally starts with the detox program. After that comes a long term inpatient treatment program. Then comes long term after care. After care is a good twelve to eighteen months long, While going to the outpatient treatment program you will also need to be attending AA or NA weekly support groups. It took a long time for you to get to this point in your addiction and there is no easy way out. During and after this eighteen months of after care you will most likely be going to one on one counseling. When you start your AA or NA meetings you will need a sponsor. The best way to use a sponsor is to call them every Monday and Friday nights. You call every Monday and Friday for two years. When you call you can just tell the sponsor, “Hi, I am doing fine, we will see you at the meeting.” The reason for this is because if you get used to calling your sponsor when you don’t need them, you will call them when you do need them. You must keep away from all people, places, and things from the old life. It is good to work towards a goal that you always thought you could never achieve whwn you were using your drugs and or alcohol. You may start taking classes towards something you always wanted to do. Keep yourself clean, sober, happy, and productive.

FROM ADDICTION TO RECOVERY

STEP 1. DEFINING THE DYSFUNCTIONAL LIFESTYLE OF ADDICTION.

1 ADDICTION
2 HOMELESSNESS
3 JOBLESSNESS
4 FAMILY REJECTION
5 LOSS OF ALL FRIENDS
6 MENTAL BREAKDOWN
7 HEALTH PROBLEMS
8 MORAL BREAKDOWN
9 BROKEN FAMILIES
10 LEGAL PROBLEMS
11 REJECTION FROM FRIENDS
12 LOSS OF ALL PRIDE
13 NO SELF-ESTEEM
14 LOSS OF ALL HOPE
15 SUICIDAL THOUGHTS

STEP 2. WHAT ARE THE FEARS OF RECOVERY? THESE FEARS ARE REAL TO THE PERSON, BUT IN REALITY THEY ARE NOT REAL AT ALL.

1 FEAR OF SUCCESS
2 FEAR OF FAILURE
3 FEAR OF CHANGE
4 FEAR OF REALITY
5 FEAR OF OBLIGATIONS
6 FEAR OF RESPONSIBILITY
7 FEAR OF YOURSELF
8 FEAR OF FACING FAMILY & RELATIVES
9 FEAR OF PENDING LEGAL ISSUES
10 FEAR OF REJECTION & ACCEPTANCE

STEP 3, THE CHARACTERISTICS OF A CLEAN AND SOBER LIFESTYLE. YOU MUST PUT YOUR HEART, GUT, BLOOD AND SOAL INTO YOUR LIFE OF RECOVERY INORDER FOR IT TO WORK.

1 BEING RESPONSIBLE
2 KEEPING FOCUSED ON SELF AND RECOVERY
3 DEALING WITH THE SKELETONS IN THE CLOSET
4 MAINTAINING A GOO SUPPORT SYSTEM
5 BEING OPEN MINDED
6 BEING EMPATHETIC TOWARDS OTHERS
7 LEARNING TO FINISH WHAT WE START
8 DEVELOPING GOOD LIVING SKILLS
9 DEVELOPING POSITIVE CLEAN AND SOBER FRIENDS IN RECOVERY
10 SETTING POSITIVE STRONG BOUNDARIES FOR YOURSELF
11 LEARNING YOUR RED FLAGS
12 BEING PATIENT WITH THE FAMILIES FEAR OF YOUR RELAPSE
13 LEARNING TO KEEP THINKING POSITIVE

STEP 4, THE TOOLS FOR EARLY RECOVERY

1 AA/NA MEETINGS
2 OUTPATIENT OR INPATIENT TREATMENT PROGRAMS
3 COUNSELING
4 GETTING A SPONSOR AND LEARNING TO USE THEM
5 KEEPING AWAY FROM ALL OLD PEOPLE, PLACES, AND THINGS FROM THE OLD LIFESTYLE
6 DEVELOPING A SUPPORT TEAM
7 WORKING TOWARDS GOALS THAT SEEMED IMPOSSIBLE BEFORE RECOVERY
8 EDUCATION, TAKING CLASSES TOWARDS BETTERING JOB SKILLS
9 LEARNING TO LIVE DAILY BY THE GOLDEN RULES OF RECOVERY

[GOLDEN RULES OF RECOVERY: CLEAN, SOBER, HAPPY & PRODUCTIVE]

DANGEROUS FEELINGS & EMOTIONS IN EARLY RECOVERY

EMOTIONS CAN BE VERY DANGEROUS IN EARLY RECOVERY

When a person first steps into a life of recovery from many years of addiction, they are unaware of many feelings and emotions that are normal to other people. People that have never been afflicted with the problem of drugs and alcohol taking over their lives have no idea what we are talking about. To the person that is new in recovery from ten to twenty years of a hard addiction these otherwise normal feeling and emotions are very new to him or her. The most common problem with people new in recovery is isolation. Because they are not used to this new life of recovery, they shun from others and try to just be a loner. This brings on many feelings and emotions like depression, lost and out of place, loneliness, anxiety, and even aggression. With these people not seeking profession help; they do not know how to deal with these new problems. Working close with a sponsor helps a whole lot but there is another problem and that is the fear of asking a stranger to be your sponsor. Many people in very early recovery do not want to go around asking someone to be a sponsor so they think they will just do this by themselves. This brings on the isolation and more problems. They start feeling stress and depression when they run into problems and complications and they feel they have nobody to turn to. These complications cause most people in very early recovery to relapse. These relapses are because these people get so lonely and feel totally out of place that they just return to the lifestyle they are very used to. Many relapses could be prevented if the older ones in recovery would do their job better. They need to reach out right away to new people helping them make the transition from the life of addiction to the life of sobriety.

Forty to fifty years ago most people in early recovery were in recovery from alcohol only. The times have changed now and most all people in early recovery are in recovery from multiple addictions. The average person is in recovery from two, three, or maybe more drugs at the same time. In this modern day, these people start using drugs and alcohol much earlier in life than people did forty to fifty years ago. Most of these people were well on their way to a very serous addiction by the time they were thirteen to fourteen years old. These active addictions would sometimes stay with them for life. They would never get the chance to experience these feeling and emotions in normal life until they would enter recovery from drugs and alcohol. When these people at the age of thirty, forty, or fifty years old start experiencing these feelings and emotions, without professional help, it can cause family problems. The family members start feeling the anger from these people when they have nobody to turn to for guidance. To many of these, people they have stepped into the unknown, a lifestyle they have never experienced before.

If you are attending a good outpatient program, you will be able to get all the help you need. The outpatient treatment is where they will be working with a rehabilitation specialist that will teach them about these new feeling and emotions they will start having and how to deal with them. The rehabilitation specialist will work closely with them to help them through the major problems of early recovery. When a person starts looking for a good outpatient treatment program, there are questions they should ask. Do not be afraid to ask to see their certifications and license numbers. There is a world of difference between a counselor and a Certified Rehabilitation Specialist. The Certified Rehabilitation Specialist is an expert in all areas of addiction and recovery. They are also able to help the family through these rough times. Below is a chart that shows the eight dangerous feeling and emotions of early recovery.

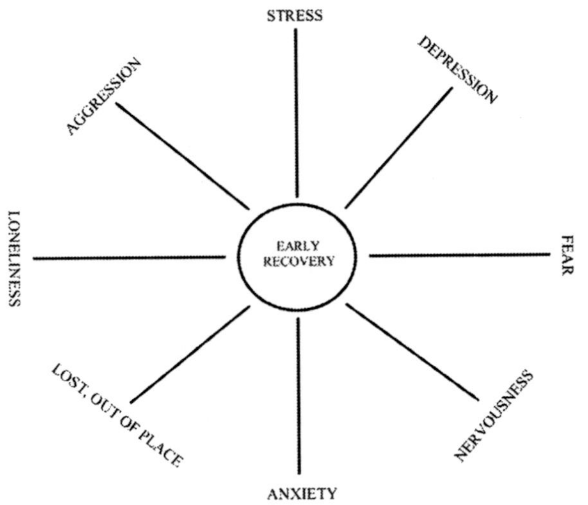

THESE FEELINGS COME FROM THE PERSON STEPPING INTO A LIFE OF SOBRIETY THAT TO THEM IS A NEW LIFE AND A NEW WAY TO LIVE. WHEN WE STEP INTO THE UNKNOWN THESE FEELINGS ARE VERY NORMAL. HOW WE RESPOND TO THESE FEELING WILL DETERMINE IF THE OUTCOME WILL BE POSITIVE OR NEGATIVE.

THE BUILDING BLOCKS OF RECOVERY

THE FOUNDATION

We all start in rebuilding our lives as soon as we start our first day of recovery from a long addiction with eight major areas. We must start with the foundation. This the most important part in our life of recovery. This block must be maintained at all cost. It is the weekly support system, the outpatient treatment program, and the one on one counseling you will receive in the eighteen months of after care. After you have completed your eighteen months after care, you will need to maintain this block for the rest of your life.

STABLE HOUSING

Many people new in recovery start with the Mission, or a local shelter. While in the shelter they will continue their weekly support system and start working on getting a job or other form of income like SSI. They will also be working on some stable housing for themselves. There are several types of housing program. Some counties have much better housing programs than others do. The local shelter, detox units, and missions are all well informed of the housing programs in their areas.

MEDICAL/MENTAL HEALTH NEEDS

One of the major problems of addiction is that for ten, fifteen or twenty years we live through a bad addiction to drugs and alcohol we rarely go to see a doctor. It is very important for us to start getting medical treatment right away and possibly mental health care also. The years of active addiction cause several medical problems that can be corrected or arrested with medical treatment.

TRAINING OR EDUCATION

Due to the problem of being out of the job market for years, we find we really do not have any job skills at all. We are at the stage in life where we cannot do hard labor for work because of our age and or health. It is good at this time to be trained for a new type of work, or perhaps start at a local community collage taking classes towards a certification in a field you would really like to work in. School counselors are able to help in this area.

CLEAN UP OLD LEGAL PROBLEMS

Most everyone that goes into recovery from years of addiction, find themselves facing one or several legal problems they acquired during their years of using drugs and alcohol. These issues must be cleared up in order for the person to move on with their life of sobriety. It is always good to gain the help of a Rehabilitation Specialist to assist you in this process. They will know how to help you gain as much support as possible before you go into court to face a judge. Most of the time when a judge can see you have been in treatment, continuing in outpatient follow-up care, and receiving on going counseling they get very easy on their restitution for the past legal problems.

REUNITE WITH FAMILY

There comes a time when we must go back and face the family members that for years we stole from, abused, and mistreated during our addiction. Many time people wait until they have a year or so clean and sober so they would have something good to tell them when they see them. This is not required. The best time to start contacting the family is right away. Keep them updated on your progress. Do not be discouraged at their negative attitude towards you because when you go into recovery, they go into recovery also. It is good for the family members to get counseling. You could even have your counselor make the first contact with your family members. There are many ways, and a lot of help to deal with this issue.

There are three stages to the life of drug and alcohol use. There are Use, Abuse, and Addiction. We start with the use of drugs and alcohol until we start getting dependant of the drugs and alcohol. We than graduate to the abuse stage of drugs and alcohol and we stay at this stage sometimes for years. Then we graduate to the addiction stage of drugs and alcohol. We can stay at this final stage for many years until it takes us so low in life that we wander if we are really alive or not. Many people will die at this stage and many of us will get help and proceed into recovery. When we start into the building of our lives in recovery we sometimes get in to much of a hurry and we want to get the six most important areas of our building blocks of recovery done right now. This cannot be done. It may take months before we are able to get the six areas all in order. We can only start with the most important one first, the foundation. A good counselor will be able to help you along and will make sure you are not going too fast. It took many years for you to get to this point in your life. It will not be fixed overnight.

As you are going through the first six areas of our building blocks of recovery, we find that it does not stop after the first six. These six are just starting the process. As we continue in our life of sobriety, we keep adding to out pyramid of recovery. Going to school and getting better skilled is great. This is another block added to your pyramid. We may someday buy a home, as we progress in life our pyramid keeps getting bigger and bigger. We have to always remember that our first block is always the most important and must always be kept up, at all cost. If we fail to maintain our support system all we have built will crumble. Everything we build over the years can be lost in a moment.

THE BUILDING BLOCKS OF RECOVERY

TRAINING/EDUCATION   LEGAL ISSUES   REUNITE WITH FAMILY

STABLE HOUSING   MEDICAL & MENTAL

WEEKLY SUPPORT
[FOUNDATION]

AS WE GROW IN RECOVERY WE AD TO OUR PYRAMID OR RECOVERY

SCHOOL EDUCATION   MARRIAGE FAMILY   BUYING A HOME   PLANNING FOR A RETIREMENT

TRAINING/ EDUCATION   CLEANUP LEGAL ISSUES   REUNITE WITH FAMILY

STABLE HOUSING   MEDICAL & MENTAL

WEEKLY SUPPORT
[FOUNDATION]

DOMESTIC VIOLENCE & ADDICTION

YOU WILL FIND THERE IS MUCH MORE INFORMATION ON THE INTERNET ON DOMESTIC VIOLENCE

Domestic violence and addiction fit together hand in hand. Most all cases of domestic violence in this country are associated with heavy drug and alcohol use and abuse. The three types of abuse are Physical, Sexual, and Mental abuse. The abuser uses the abuse as a means of maintaining total control over everybody in the family. The one that gets the most abuse is normally the wife or girlfriend. As time goes on the abuse will increase to the point that the abused starts fighting for her life. In many cases, the abused will start using alcohol and drugs as a painkiller or medication to help with the pains of the abuse. The abuse continues until it reaches the point where the abused person starts to become numb to the physical abuse but the mental abuse gets to the critical point. The abused person's only goal is to protect her children.

The abused person may reach the point where they end up killing the abuser. This is the emotion of Terror, Total Insanity, and Rage. All three are released within the abused person at the same moment. There is no way possible for any person to maintain any control over their actions when all three of these emotions are being released at the same moment. At this moment, the abused person is in a state of complete temporary insanity and totally out of control of himself or herself. It can sometimes seem like an injustice when these victims of massive abuse are charged with first-degree murder. They were probably raised in family units where alcohol, drugs, and abuse were a common part of everyday life. Their whole life has been one big nightmare and this is why many abused people find suicide to be an acceptable way out of this nightmare.

There is a way out for the abused wife and children. There are many hide-a-way houses being set up all the time where these victims can go to and feel safe. A victim can go to any detox, counselor, police officer, public service worker, and let them know they need help to get out of this life of nightmares. There is BWA, Battered Women's Association, this is a very powerful organization in our country. It has been fighting domestic violence for many years. There are child specialists and counselors that will be able to help until the abused family is able to maintain on their own. There have been cases where the abuser killed his family and committed suicide. I feel that this action happens when the abuser starts finding that he is loosing total control over the abused person and feels they have no other course of action. Even when the abused person does break away and starts a new life, it is usually years before they can even think of starting a new more positive relationship. Many abused women that do break away and get help will look at all men as abusers for a very long time. With the proper help, this can be corrected. The children growing up in this lifestyle adapt this as a normal way to live.

I have worked with clients that have a long history as abusers and they would say, "Bitches are to be controlled". They would get very upset when I would ask them what about the man that comes along and feels the same way towards your own daughter? This would really get them thinking. I would ask them if they would like their son to grow up thinking and feeling that way. A couple of questions really bring it home for the abuser if you start bringing their own families into the picture. The abuser can get help also but it is a long process. At times the abuser has got to leave the family unit while he is getting this long-term help. This does not mean the family is broken up for good, this just means that both the abused and the abuser get a little time away from each other to get the help that both are in need of. The family love and the family bond remain strong in most cases. There are many times when the family is never reunited at all. Sometimes the abused person finds there is a better life without the abuser in it. I have heard of cases from other counselors were the abuser has told his wife to go on and get a better life for herself because he feels he would just abuse her again.

DOMESTIC VIOLENCE & ADDICTION

[Profiling an abuser:]

1. A push for quick involvement [to develop a quick relationship].

2. Jealousy

3. Verbal abusiveness: Constantly criticizes you, saying hurtful things, calling you ugly names.
   You wonder, "What's wrong with me? I shouldn't feel bad".

4. Controlling behavior: Questions like, where have you been, who was that on the phone, who were you with, where are you going, why didn't you call me, are just examples of controlling behavior.

5. Unrealistic expectations: Expects you to be only what he wants. Not allowing you to be yourself or to be an individual.

6. Blame others for their problems and mistakes.

7. Is frequently angry and irritable, yet claims that nothing is wrong or does not want to talk about
   It, making you think that it is ail your fault.

8. Sudden mood swings. From sweet and loving to violent in a matter of minutes, for no reason at all.

9. Isolation: Tries to cut you off from your family and friends (through criticism, & monopolizing your time. Tries to stop your success in school and work in order to keep you down and under control.

10. The abusers opinions are always right and yours are not taken into account or taken seriously, as if you don't know anything anyway.

11. What was your property is now all his, you no longer have anything of your own.

12. Use of force during sex while making you do things you do not like.

FACTS:

Physical Violence in dating relationships ranges from 20-35%.

Alcohol/drug abuse is involved in about 65 to 70% of domestic violence cases, but it is not the cause in all Domestic Violence.

Domestic violence affects all economic levels, races, and ethnic groups. There are no boundaries to domestic violence.

In most cases when the abused is using drugs and alcohol, it is being used to cover up the pain from the abuse.

About 30% of most cases of domestic violence end up in the death of either the abused or the abuser.

If it is a case of the abused killing the abuser, it is not pre-meditated. It is a moment of rage, extreme fear, and revenge. All three of these emotions engage at the same moment, causing the abused to lose all control of their actions.

WHY DO PEOPLE STAY?

Fear of being alone: An abusive relationship erodes a person's self-worth. If someone is constantly degraded and abused, they will lose their self-esteem and confidence. The abuser makes the abused feel inferior and worthless.

Psychological trauma: The abused will experience fear and confusion, preventing them from being able to break free. They learn to accept this abusive treatment if it were "normal" and lose confidence that they can act in defense of themselves.

Shame: People are afraid of what others might think or say. They experience a sense of shame and failure if they are given the responsibility for the relationship. They fear the stigma a break-up and domestic violence brings. People feel shame and guilt for leaving. They think they must make the relationship work.

Denial: People are brainwashed and confused. They believe that they deserve the abusive treatment because their perception of reality clashes with what their abuser tells them. "That it is all her fault." They do not want to be labeled as victims. Denial is a great place to be under these circumstances.

Fear of retaliation: The abused fear the abuser will retaliate against them. Becoming more aggressive, seeking revenge, if they attempt to leave. They do not want to create more problems or a higher risk for them and the family.

Lack of financial resources: People do not think that they could make it on their own because they have always been financially dependent on their partner.

SOLUTIONS

Support groups or counseling can help to regain confidence and know that she/he is not alone. Getting encouragement and reassurance enable she/he to know that they are not inferior but equal.

Support groups can help an abused person realize that they do not deserve this bad treatment. The abuser is the one with the problem. The abused person will have the comfort and safety in the support group or with a counselor that they lack from the abuser.

Support groups or counseling can help people realize that their safety and happiness is much more important than they realized. Counseling will help them realize that they are not responsible for the irrationality of others.

Support groups or counseling will encourage people to recognize the problem and learn to trust their own perceptions and judgments encouraging them to take action for themselves.

Get a restraining order for protection. Stay away from places where the abuser usually goes. Stay with someone that can be trusted and that the abuser does not know. Do not tell him/her you are thinking about leaving. Most abusers do not change, but to get worse and more violent.

Locate temporary work, financial aid for school, emergency shelters, emergency loans, roommate housing, support from family and friends.

THE ROLE OF ALCOHOL & DRUGS IN DOMESTIC VIOLENCE SITUATIONS

About 3 million violent crimes occur each year in which victims perceived the offenders to have been drinking and using drugs at the time of the offense. Among those victims who provided information about the offenders use of alcohol and drugs, about 35% of the victimizations involved an offender who had been drinking or on drugs. Two-thirds of victims who suffered violence by an intimate [or former spouse, boyfriend, or girlfriend] reported that alcohol and drugs had been a factor. Among spouse victims, 8 out of 10 incidents were reported to have involved an offender who had been drinking or using drugs. By contrast, an estimated 36% of stranger victimizations were determined that alcohol and/or drugs were being used by the abused. On average, their husbands or boyfriends in this country murder more than 15 women everyday. In the year 2000, intimate partners killed about 2500 women. In the same year, victims or partners killed about 450 men. Women are much more likely than men to be killed by an intimate partner. In the year 2000, intimate partner homicides accounted for about 35 percent of the murders of women and less than four percent of the murders of men.

FROM A MEDICATION TO AN ADDICTION

In most of the detoxification and treatment programs for drug & alcohol treatment for women, you will find most of these women were victims of a lifetime of domestic violence. Many of these women were victims of severe physical abuse. Many women in treatment for addiction started using alcohol and drugs as a medication to help them deal and cope with everyday physical and mental abuse. Self-medication soon becomes a necessity and the use soon becomes an active addiction. Now the use of drugs and alcohol is serving a dual purpose. That is to both medicate for the physical and mental abuse, and to maintain the addiction. The children soon become less important in her everyday life and secondary to the job of maintaining the addiction. The needs of the family soon become secondary issues to the number one priority, which is to maintain the daily addiction.

THE BATTLE FOR THE DRUGS & ALCOHOL

There soon becomes another big problem in the family now that both the father and mother are addicted to drugs and alcohol. The violence soon changes because the woman may now result to violence herself to maintain her addiction. This violence from her may be directed towards her children or her husband, whichever gets in the way of maintaining her daily addiction. This will soon raise the level of violence in the family unit. The woman now becomes the giver of violence as well as the receiver of violence. She can, and does in most cases, take on the same characteristics of the abusive husband. The children receive the essentials needed to get by, while the rest of the family resources go to maintaining dads and then mom's addictions. This severe victim abuse has now been passed on to the children.

REALITY SETS IN

The woman is now torn because she is now abusing her own children. She tried so hard to protect them from the domestic violence and now they have become her own victims. The domestic violence towards her has not stopped at all. It has even escalated, but her awareness of it has changed. She is not so concerned about the abuse towards her as she is about the issue of maintaining her own addiction. Still in the back of her mind, her love for her children and her will to protect them is still strong. It has just been distorted by the active addiction. Once she goes into treatment and recovery, she will experience powerful guilt. There will be a need for a lot of counseling and therapy to overcome this guilt. She will come to understand that addiction is so powerful it can make you reach this level. She will soon understand that her self-medicating became an addiction and took control over her life. She will be able to see how she came to have the one thing that she hated about her husband, addiction. This will also help her to understand the power of the addiction in her husband and how the violence played a big part in the dysfunctional family unit. This whole process can become a powerful tool for the recovery of the family unit.

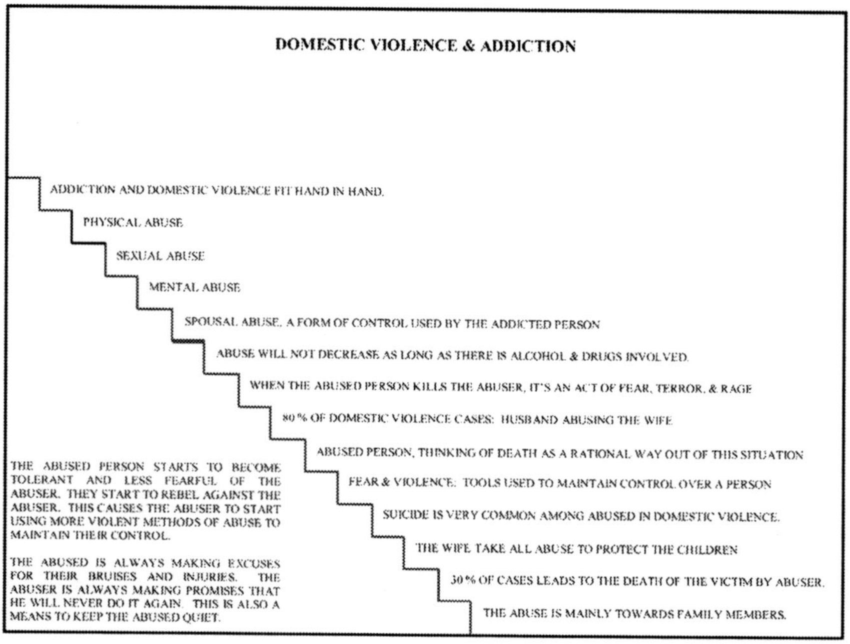

THE EFFECTS OF COCAINE ON THE HUMAN BODY

A DEATH SENTENCE TO OUR KIDS

Cocaine/Crack has an overwhelming effect on the pleasure centers in the brain. The drug interferon, alters, damages, and takes control of specialized cells in the brain that regulate pleasure, the sense of well-being, and moods. Regular use of cocaine may disable the brain's ability to feel normal without cocaine. Long-term use will ensure an addiction, which will take a long time and a lot of work to get over. Cocaine/Crack can damage the liver's ability to detoxify blood while reducing production of crucial enzymes needed for normal body functions. Hepatitis can be contracted and cause serious liver damage, cirrhosis, and liver cancer. Hepatitis is highly contagious. Cocaine/Crack can cause main blood arteries to constrict and causing blockage in the main heart arteries, causing heart attacks and or death. Cocaine/Crack can cause problems of the reproductive system for men and women and could cause birth deformities. It will also cause high blood pressure at a very young age.

Cocaine/Crack use by pregnant women can cause miscarriages, developmental disorders, and complications during birth. It can result in premature birth or stillbirth. Adults using cocaine/crack can result in their having a crack baby, in need of detoxification after birth. These babies run a greater risk of Sudden Infant Death Syndrome, SIDS. Cocaine babies have a higher risk of respiratory and kidney trouble along with visual problems, lack of coordination, and retardation. These babies are prone to suffer strokes and heart attacks. Cocaine/Crack can be very damaging to the lungs of the crack and cocaine smoker. Cocaine/Crack users stand a very high risk of contracting several types of diseases. Some of the most common ones are Hepatitis C, D & E, as well as the AIDS virus. There is treatment with various degrees of success, but no cure yet. There are some other types is illnesses that can be almost as deadly.

Cocaine/Crack is so addictive that the more you use the more you have to have. These are other problems when people smoke cocaine/crack around babies and young children. The second hand smoke from crack and cocaine that babies and young children inhale can cause them to start a craving for the drug at a very young age. Cocaine/Crack is the drug most commonly used by the kids in school and most of these kids got the idea of using this drug from their parents or peers. Cocaine/Crack is the drug that is most commonly available to the children in school. These school kids using this drug are lead into steeling and committing other crimes in order to be able to keep on the drugs. It leads these kids into prostitution at a very young age. Prostitution can lead them to get Hepatitis C, D, E and AIDS before they are even eighteen years old. Once these kids get any of the illnesses that cannot be cured, they think their life is over and many cases end in suicide. The financial strain that cocaine/crack use puts on the family unit can be devastating and very destructive to the family unit. Family members addicted to cocaine/crack end up steeling money and valuables from family, friends, or from anybody they can. They have to keep that addiction maintained no matter what.

THE HARMFUL EFFECTS OF COCAINE & CRACK ON THE BODY

BRAIN, EUPHORIA [HAPPY & PLEASANT] AND DEPRESSION Early effects include euphoria lasting 5 to 15 minutes. This "high" is followed by a crushing "low" [depression] that leaves user craving more of the drug. **BRAIN DAMAGE & ADDICTION** Cocaine & crack have an overwhelming effect on the pleasure centers in the brain. The drug interfere, alters, damage, and take control of specialized cells that regulate pleasure, well-being, and mood. Regular use may shut off brains ability to ever be or feel normal without cocaine. Long term use will cause permanent addiction that will take a long time and a lot of work to break.	**LIVER** Cocaine and crack can damage liver's ability to detoxify blood, while reducing production of crucial enzymes needed for normal body functions. Hepatitis can be contracted and cause serious liver damage, lead to cirrhosis and liver cancer. Hepatitis is highly contagious and can be passes on to others. **INTESTINES** Blood supply is reduced to intestines, resulting in nausea, diarrhea, painful cramps, inflammation, and possible death. **BLOOD VESSELS** Cocaine and crack causes blood vessels to contract, increasing blood pressure and risk of heart attack and stroke.	**REPRODUCTIVE SYSTEM MALES & FEMALES** Regular use can result in loss of interest in sex, and decreased sexual performance. **PREGNANCY & UNBORN BABIES** Cocaine and crack causes miscarriages, developmental disorders, and complications during birth. Can redult in premature birth or stillbirths. Parents using cocaine & crack can result in the baby being a crack baby, needing detoxifacation after birth. Babies run greater risk of **Sudden Infant Death Syndrome [SIDS].** Cocaine babies have higher risk of respiratory, kidney trouble, visual problems, lack of coordination, and retardation Babies can suffer stroke and heart attacks **BODY WEIGHT** Loss of appetite can be so severe that it leads to dramatic weight loss and malnutrition..	**PSYCHOLOGICAL & PERSONALITY CHANGES** Irritability, anxiety, panic attacks, excitable, hyper, erratic, confussed, depressed, non-stop babbling, sleepless-ness, chronic fatigue, short tempers, aggressness, violent, suicidal behaviors, overly suspicious, have delusions, paranoia, and hallucinations are common symptoms. **EYES** Dilation of pupils, vision blurred. **THROAT** Inhaling cocain vapors causes hoarse-ness, caughing and constant sore throat. **LUNGS** Smoking cocaine damages lung cells ability to process gases leaving user with constant cough and short of breath. Use may result in respiratory failure.	**HEART** Constricts heart's blood vessels, increasing blood pressure. This may trigger heart attack, heart failure, irregular heart beat, and sudden death. **TRANSMITTING DISEASES** Users sharing needles run the high risk of infecting themselves with hepatitis or deadly AIDS. Users may pass these diseases to other sexual partners or unborn babies. **ADDED DANGERS: COCAETHYLENE** When people mix cocaine and alcohol consumption, they are compounding the danger each drug poses and unknowingly forming a complex chemical experiment within their bodies. The human liver combines cocaine and alcohol and manufactures a third substance, cocaethylene, that intensifies alcohol & cocaine's effects, while possibly increasing the risk of sudden death.
CENTRAL NERVOUS SYSTEM Increases blood presure, heart rate, breathing, and body temperature. Suppresses desire for food, sex, and sleep. Can cause stroke, brean seizures, respiratory failure, heart attack, convulsions, and death	**SECOND-HAND COCAINE SMOKE AROUND BABIES AND CHILDREN** Babies and children breathing secone-hand cocaine smoke causes physical damage to their continued growing bodies and could cause their bodies to start craving the drug.	**SOCIAL DECLINE OF THE LIFESTYLE** The longer the person uses cocaine the more they have to use each time. This puts a big financial burdon on the whole family unit. The users cravings get so strong that the financial situation of the family unit is no longer a concern.		

ALCOHOL AND THE HUMAN BODY

Alcohol affects most all of the parts of the human body. It damages the central nervous system and causes major damage to the short-term memory we rely on in every day life. After many years of heavy addiction, alcohol starts causing liquids to build up in the lungs causing pneumonia and scaring of the lung tissue. Over continued heavy use the person would die of pneumonia or drowning in his or her own fluids. Hepatitis, Cirrhosis of the Liver, Scarred Tissue, Yellow Jaundice is the main liver problems that come with heavy alcohol use, abuse, and addiction. Any of these are fatal with continued alcohol use and without proper medical treatment. Pregnancy and alcohol use does not go together. The baby could be born with Fetal Alcohol Syndrome, possible brain damage, poor muscles, speech disorders, and retarded growth development. Over many years of alcohol abuse, you could start having very dangerous alcohol seizures. This is when every cell in the body goes crazy at the same time. You do not remember anything at all. Your body becomes stiff and hard as a board. If this seizure continues for several minutes, you could suffer permanent brain damage or death.

These seizures are very dangerous. There has been people that have had an alcoholic seizure by themselves and were later found dead from of the seizure. If a person has a very bad heart, it could trigger heart attacks right along with the seizure. You could get pancreatic and permanent kidney damage that will result in you living on a machine for the rest of your life. Alcohol causes the heart to enlarge and causes blood on the brain. Blood on the brain is, when blood builds up between the brain and the skull. It will cause bleeding ulcers that could be fatal.

ALCOHOL'S EFFECTS ON THE HUMAN BODY

BRAIN & CENTRAL NERVOUS SYSTEM	LUNGS	LIVER	PREGNANCY & UN-BORN BABIES	OTHER COMMON FUNCTIONS	MAJOR BODY FUNCTIONS	INTESTINES
IMPAIRED BEHAVIOR, JUDGEMENT, MEMORY, CONCENTRATION,AND COORDINATION Drinking impairs regions of the brain controlling behavior and emotions. Alcohol induces extreme mood swings and emotional outburst. **BRAIN DAMAGE & EFFECTS** Alcohol acts as a sedative on the central nervous system depressing the nerve cells in the brain, dulling, altering,, and damaging their ability to respond. Large doses can cause heavy sleep, respiratory failure, coma, and death **BRAIN DISORDERS & ADDICTION** Long term drinking may result in permanent brain damage, serious mental disorders, and addiction to alcohol,	Large amounts of alcohol could cause breathing to stop, and possible death. It lowers the resistance and could cause infections in the lungs. Over long-term heavy use it will cause the lungs to start filling with liquids causing pneumonia and scaring of the lung tissue.	**CHRONIC HEAVY DRINKING**. may cause alcoholic hepatitis and destruction of lever cells and then cirrhosis lesions, resulting total destruction of the liver. Impairs the liver's ability to remove yellow pigment and the skin appears yellow, known as yellow jaundice. Liver damage causes fluids to build in extremities through out the body Decreases production of blood-clotting factors, may cause uncontrolled bleeding. Liver accumulates fat which can cause liver failure, coma, and death.	**DRINKING DURING PREGNANCY**. significantly increases chance of delivering a baby with fetal alcohol syndrome, small head, possible brain damage, abnormal facial features, poor muscle tone, speech and sleep disorders, and retarded growth and development.	**EYES,** Distorted vision and ability to adjust to lights, pinpoint pupils, and red eyes. **EARS** Diminishes ability to distinguish between sounds and perceives their directions. **MOUTH** Slurred speech, dulls taste and smell, reducing desire to eat. **THROAT** Irritation and damage to lining of esophagus, induces severe vomiting, hemorrhaging, pain and difficulty swallowing, cancer. **MUSCLES** Muscles become weaker and can cause pain, spasms and tenderness	**HEART** Weakens the heart muscles and ability to pump. Causes heart enlargement, abnormal heart signs and irregular heart beats. **STOMACH** Irritation to stomach lining, peptic ulcers, inflammation, bleeding, and cancer **PANCREAS** Significant risk to pancreatis, and chronic inflammation of the pancreas.	Irritation of the lining of the intestinal track and colon, Chronic drinking may result in inflammation, ulcers, and cancer of intestines and colon. Nausea, diarrhea, vomiting, sweating, and loss of appetite, are common. Alcohol impairs small intestine's ability to process nutrients and vitamins. **BONES** Alcohol interferes with the body's ability to absorb calcium resulting in bones being weak, soft, brittle, and thinner.
OTHER AFFECTS ON CENTRAL NERVOUS SYSTEM Impaired visual ability. Unclear hearing. Dulled smell & taste. Lose of pain perception. Altered sense of time & space Impaired fine motor skills Slow reactions Impaired sexual performance						

THE DORMANT OR RELAPSE ZONE

After we have cleared a detox unit and completed an inpatient treatment program, we go back into an everyday normal life. We have all the greatest intentions on maintaining a strong support system and living clean and sober. After you are home for a week or two, some people still have not started attending any AA or NA meetings to establish their life long support system. This opens the door to stinking thinking, "*why attend all those meeting? I am not drinking or using, I am doing just fine without them. I will just not drink or use and do this on my own*". What these people have done is stop at the <u>Dormant Zone or Relapse Zone.</u> This is a place where we feel safe and comfortable for a short time. We think we can just stay here. This is just an illusion of sobriety. Many people that are stuck here time after time cannot ever seem to accept the fact that in order to make it they have to go all the way into sobriety. These people want the all the blessings sobriety has to offer, but they are not willing to do what they will have to do to gain these blessings. This zone leads you to the marry-go-round to hell. This is sober one week, and drunk and wasted the next week, week-in-week-out. We can never reach true sobriety in this zone.

From this zone, we find we are hanging with the old people, places & things. Most everything we do and think is related to the old lifestyle and not even close to a life of sobriety. You must go all the way into the life of sobriety, the support system, and the whole works. While working in the detox units for many years, I have found many clients with a long record of having to detox every three to six weeks. Some of these people have been doing this for years. After talking to many of these clients, I noticed that every one of these people fell into this dormant zone trap. They just would not accept the fact that this big problem is due to the choices they have been making. If a person afflicted with addiction cannot accept the fact that they have to maintain a support system for the rest of their lives they will keep falling into this dormant zone. Sadly, some people die by addiction because they just cannot accept this at all. As long as these people stay in this dormant zone, their internal organs continue to take a beating. They loose their ability to function normally and soon have major medical problems and maybe death. The family unit continues to suffer as long as these people keep going back every time to this dormant zone.

When a person steps into recovery from addiction, they will be either one of two types of people. They will go into a good strong life of sobriety with a good weekly support system or they will return to their life of addiction. What I am trying to say is that the dormant zone really does not exist at all, only in the person's mind. The dormant zone is in reality a zone of false safety that is nothing more than returning to their life of addiction. Some people that relapse repeatedly would tell me they go to church every Sunday and that is their support system. I am a strong Christian. Gong to church every Sunday will not keep me clean and sober. It has nothing to do with maintaining a weekly support system. A good strong weekly support system is attending AA or NA meetings every week, being around other people in recovery, and maintaining a life of sobriety. Going to church is a great thing but it is not a weekly support system. If this is what you choose to do, you will keep on relapsing. After many years of sobriety, some people can just attend church as a continued support but these are people that have many years of solid sobriety established in their lives. For people in early recover, you have to jump through the hoops, and give it your heart, blood and soul, for many years.

RELAPSE PREVENTION
RELAPSE DANGER ZONE
THE DORMANT ZONE

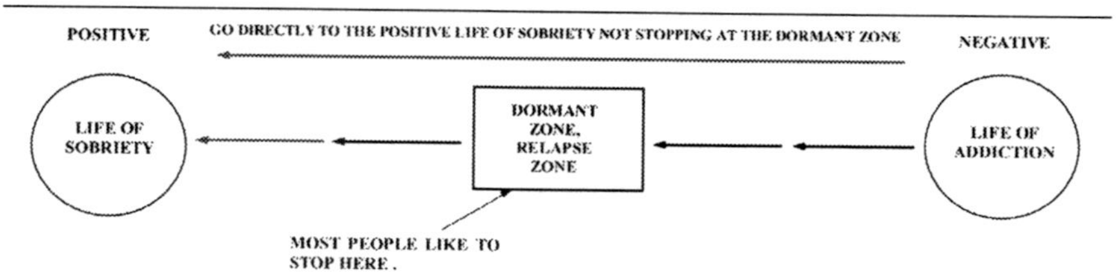

WHEN WE STEP INTO A LIFE OF SOBRIETY AND WE STOP USING THE DRUGS AND ALCOHOL THERE BECOMES A BIG VOID IN OUT LIVES. THIS VOID IS AN EMPTINESS THAT IS CAUSED WHEN WE GET CLEAN AND SOBER. IF WE STOP IN THE DORMANT ZONE AND NEVER GO ALL THE WAY INTO THE POSITIVE LIFE THIS VOID NEVER GETS FILLED.

AS THIS VOID GETS STRONGER AND STRONGER WE SOON FELL DESPERATE TO FILL IT WITH ANYTHING. IF WE ARE STUCK IN THE DORMANT ZONE THERE IS NOTHING THERE TO FILL IT WITH SO WE START SEEKING SOMETHING TO FILL THIS VOID WITH FROM THE ONLY THING WE KNOW, THE OLD LIFE, AND THE OLD PEOPLE, PLACES, AND THINGS.

WE LEAVE THE LIFE OF ADDICTION WITH THE BEST INTENSIONS OF GOING ALL THE WAY WITH RECOVERY & SOBRIETY. WE GET TO THE DORMANT ZONE AND FINE A FALSE CONFRONT THERE AND A FALSE SINCE OF SAFETY.

WE START FEELING LIKE THIS IS OK, I CAN JUST STAY CLEAN AND SOBER AND NOT HALF TO ATTEND THOSE MEETINGS. WE SOON FIND THAT IN THIS DORMANT ZONE WE CAN MAINTAIN SOME OF THE RELATIONSHIPS WITH THE OLD LIFESTYLE. WE FEEL SAFE WITH THIS BECAUSE WE THINK WE ARE IN RECOVERY. WE THINK WE CAN CONTROL THIS AND NOT DRINK OR USE.

WE START BY CONNECTING UP WITH A FEW OF THE OLD PEOPLE, THAN WE VISIT ONE OF THE OLD PLACES JUST ONE MORE TIME. THAN WE RETURN TO THE SAME OLD THING, A TOTAL RELAPSE.

Another way to show the dormant is by this illustration below. What this shows is a person starting into life after completing a treatment program. They will have a choice as to how they want to go into life. They could go back to a life of drugs and alcohol use and addiction. They could go into a very strong life of recovery and sobriety using a good weekly support system. They could choice the dormant zone that will lead them to the marry-go-round to hell. This life starts out good and goes down hill very fast. We are playing games with our sobriety when we choice this path. The thing to always remember is that if we do not maintain a strong support system and we do relapse we get to go back and start at the beginning all over again.

It is always good to go right into an outpatient treatment program for twelve months or longer right after we have completed a long-term inpatient treatment program. The Rehabilitation Specialist will help you along the way keeping you from taking the wrong path in sobriety. This does not mean you will be attending groups five nights a week in an outpatient treatment program. Most rehabilitation specialist or counselors will take into consideration that the person has just completed an intense program and set them up with a couple meetings per week along with their weekly AA or NA meetings. The dormant zone is the easy way out but very costly in a week or so because it is not real. It is a zone where we do feel good for a very short time. In this zone, we do not associate with other people in recovery. We end up associating with the same people we left when we went into the inpatient treatment program at the start. These old people places and things are very glad to see you because they know you have money in your pocket.

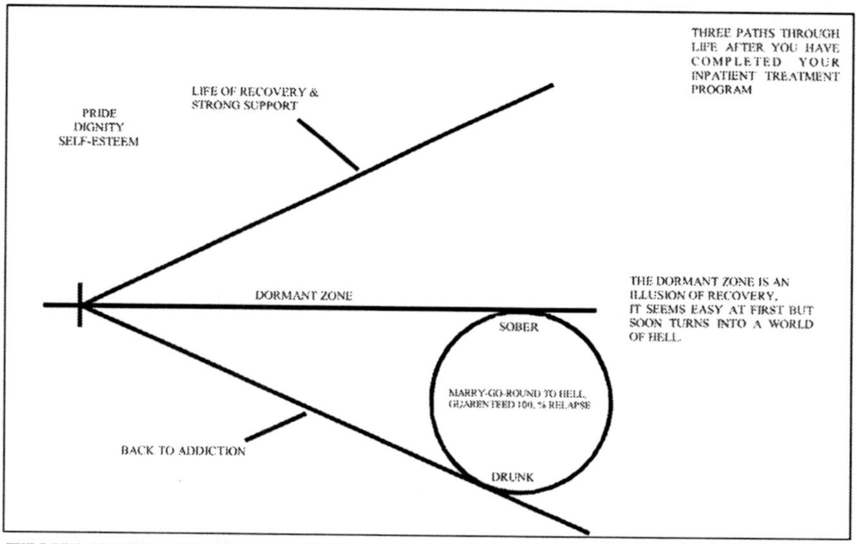

THE DORMANT ZONE, I DON'T WANT TO ATTEND ALL THOSE MEETINGS, I WILL JUST NOT USE OR DRINK. I CAN DO THIS BY MYSELF, WHY DO I NEED ALL THIS CRAP. I GOT BETTER THINGS TO DO WITH MY TIME THAN ATTEND A BUNCH OF MEETINGS.

THE DORMANT ZONE LEADS TO 100% GUARENTEED RELAPSE EVERY TIME, DON'T JOKE AROUND WITH IT.

CHAPTER 5

THE SEVENTEEN MOST COMMON EXCUSES FOR RELAPSE

The easiest thing in life for an addicted person in early recovery to do is to find a reason to relapse. On the other hand if we are looking for a reason to relapse that means there is something wrong with our recovery and support system, or maybe the reason why we went into recovery. One thing that most people in recovery never realize is that there are two parts to a good weekly support system. The first part is the serious part. This is the outpatient treatment program, AA and NA groups, twelve step group's, one on one counseling, or any other support group that gives us the knowledge we need to stay clean and sober. The other part to the weekly support system is the fun or enjoyment part of our life of sobriety. This is the clean and sober dances, potluck dinners thrown by AA, AA camping trips, a night out with other clean and sober friends, and a lot more. This makes attending a weekly support system a lot of fun.

By keeping up on both the serious part and the fun part or our weekly support system we start realizing that sobriety is a good life and we start enjoying it. It is impossible for any human being to just stay serious and never learn to enjoy their life of sobriety. This is where most of our sponsors fail when they start helping a newcomer getting started in a life of sobriety. Sponsors should be helping newcomers to learn to enjoy their life of sobriety as well as learning the serious things they need to learn. Trying to be nothing but serious about your recovery will only lead to burnout and relapse. Out of the seventeen most common reasons used for relapse listed below, twelve of them are because the person does not have the enjoyment side of their weekly support system going on. After reading this and the charts below and you will see that one through seventeen are all related to not learning to enjoy your life of sobriety.

It is ok to try to do ninety meetings in ninety days, but it is not ok to obligate yourself to having to. Some people will do ninety meetings in ninety days and do just fine with it. Others will find they reach the point of burnout by the time they get to meeting sixty or so. Soon after, they start reaching burnout they give up and relapse. It is better to set yourself up with five meetings a week that you will obligate yourself to attend for two years straight. After you have these five meeting a week going, if you want to try ninety in ninety days you can try it, just do not obligate yourself to do it. The goal in recovery is to be able to live clean, sober, happy, and productive. You must never forget that you can never again associate with any of the old people, places, and things. This does not mean you are now better than the old people you used to hang with at all. This does mean that because of the new positive changes in your life you cannot hang with them anymore.

As I stated before, when we were all born God gave everyone all the natural skills we would need to live a good normal life without the use of drugs or alcohol. Somewhere or somehow, we got all mixed up with addiction and this puts the natural skills we have on the back burner. Years later in life when we decide to give up the drugs and alcohol and go into recovery we start using these natural God given skills that God gave us at birth. We all have these natural life skills and the years of addiction does not make them disappear or go away. In recovery, you finally start to see who we really are and you start finding out that you have many natural skills that we never dreamed we could have. Soon we start liking the new person we found in us. It is not long and we start growing in our recovery.

LEADING UP TO A RELAPSE

[1] HALT
[2] STRESS
[3] RECOVERING FOR THE WRONG REASONS
[4] LACK OF BALANCE IN RECOVERY
[5] QUIT USING THE SUPPORT SYSTEM
[6] GRADUATION FROM RECOVERY
[7] THINGS ARE GETTING TOO GOOD
[8] LOOSING FOCUS ON SELF
[9] OLD PEOPLE, PLACES, & THINGS
[10] FORGETTING YOUR ROOTS
[11] STINKING THINKING
[12] RAPID GROWTH
[13] DISHONESTY
[14] DISCONTENT WITH SELF
[15] FEAR OF GROWTH & RECOVERY
[16] GREED
[17] WRONG PRIORITIES

IT IS ALWAYS GOOD TO READ OVER THESE AND KEEP THEM FRESH IN YOUR MIND. WHEN YOU FEEL ANY OF THESE THINGS GOING ON IN YOUR EVERY DAY LIFE, THAT IS TELLING YOU TO DO SOMETHING ABOUT IT.

IF YOU READ THESE OVER AT LEAST ONCE PER WEEK, THEY WILL BECOME A NATURAL PART OF YOUR EVERYDAY LIFE.

EDUCATIONAL MATERIAL OF STREET DRUGS

THIS AND A LOT MORE INFORMATION IS AVAILABLE ON THE INTERNET FROM MANY PROFESSIONALS WANTING TO HELP PEOPLE OVERCOME THEIR ADDICTIONS.

Methamphetamine: What is it and why is it dangerous?

Methamphetamine is a very potent central nervous system stimulant. The drug works right on the brain and spinal cord by interfering with normal neurotransmission. Neurotransmitters are chemical substances naturally produced within nerve cells used to communicate with each other and send messages to influence and regulate our thinking and all other systems throughout the body.

The main neurotransmitter affected by methamphetamine is dopamine. Dopamine is involved with our natural reward system. For example, feeling good about a job well done, getting pleasure from our family or social interactions, feeling content and that our lives are meaningful and count for something, all rely on dopamine transmission.

Methamphetamine production and use has destroyed entire communities in parts of this country, especially in the west. For drug abusers, meth has all of the attractions of the more expensive drugs and it is less expensive and far more available. In addition, like cocaine, methamphetamine devastates the user's health. It is quickly addictive and causes rapid deterioration of an abusers health, social functioning, and personal hygiene. Abusers suffer cardiovascular damage, increased risk of HIV/AIDS and a host of other life-threatening physical effects.

Methamphetamine may be inhaled, smoked, or injected. When someone starts using methamphetamine, they have increased energy, feelings of euphoria, decreased appetite, and decreased need for sleep. They also experience increased heart rate, blood pressure, sweating, restlessness, and anxiety.

Although some of these effects sound positive, they are far outweighed by the bad effects and risks of using methamphetamine. The euphoria, increased energy, and grandiosity often lead to impulsive risk-taking behaviors such as violence and sexual promiscuity. The effects of the drug can easily last twelve or more hours. Insomnia is quite common, but coming down causes depression and fatigue. Attempting to avoid depression and fatigue as well as a desire to regain the euphoria originally experienced are reasons why individuals are likely to turn to the drug again. This will make future withdrawal from the drug even harder.

One of the consequences of regular methamphetamine use, not typically seen with other drugs, is the very long recovery period. The former user experiences depression and little or no pleasure in life. Even things they once enjoyed are no longer satisfying. This inability to get pleasure from life or the environment typically lasts

2-3 years after stopping use. However, some persons never recover and remain unsatisfied due to permanent brain damage.

Brain damage could occur at least two different ways. Through dopamine depletion, over time, cells that replenish this essential neurotransmitter are destroyed. Brain damage may also occur due to increased blood pressure and heart rate, which can cause stroke and death of brain tissue. An irregular heartbeat may also lead to heart attack and even death. In addition, autopsy results of methamphetamine users document thousands of mini-strokes at the ends of microscopic blood vessels in the brain typically resulting in premature aging, and in some cases, premature senility.

WHAT IS IN METHAMPHETAMINES

Ether
Benzene
Paint Thinner
Freon
Acetone
Chloroform
Camp Stove Fuel
Starter Fluid
White Gasoline
Propane
Black Iodine
Red Devil Lye
Drano
Muriatic Acid
Battery Acid
Epson Salt
Lithium
Sodium Metal
Wooden Match heads
Cold Tablets

PCP

What is PCP?

Originally developed as a synthetic drug in 1959, Phencyclidine (PCP or angel dust) is an anesthetic. In its pure form, PCP is a white, crystalline powder. PCP, a street drug since the 1960's is now produced in clandestine labs and sometimes passed off as mescaline or as another hallucinogen with less extreme effects. In large quantities, it smells like strong ammonia. While use of PCP died down after the 70's, PCP is making resurgence in the Northeastern parts of the country despite its now known dangers. It is marketed under so many different names (wet, bobbies, dippies, dank, amp, hydro, purple haze, haze, and Lillie just to name a few) that users are not always aware that they are using it.

What does it look like, how is it used?

It is usually smoked, but PCP can be taken orally also, snorted, or injected. It is sold in capsules, tablets, powder, and liquid. Most often, the crystalline powder is sprinkled on a leafy substance, like tobacco, parsley, mint, or marijuana and then rolled into cigarettes and smoked.

What are PCP's effects when used?

The effects of PCP can be unpredictable and are often severe. Moderate doses (5 milligrams or less), generally produce initial feelings of relaxation and mild euphoria, but depression, anxiety, or disorientation can also result. Within the normal dosage range, users feel powerful, "spaced out", or detached and may experience LSD-like visual distortions. Physical effects include racing pulse, blood pressure, and body temperature, flushing and sweating, shallow breathing, numbness, and some loss of coordination. At higher doses, respiration drops and users may experience nausea, vomiting, loss of balance, and dizziness. They often display dramatic mood swings and are prone to anxiety, paranoia, and strong aggressiveness. Violent behavior is not uncommon, and the drug's ability to lower the pain threshold increases the likelihood of injury and self-mutilation. Paranoid delusions and aggressive behavior are sometimes followed by PCP-induced psychosis that may mimic symptoms of schizophrenia. Psychotic episodes can last several days, and it may take as long as two weeks for patients to return too normal. At toxic levels, or when interacting with alcohol or other depressant drugs, PCP can prove fatal, causing convulsions, coma, and respiratory arrest. PCP can also exacerbate pre-existing mental disorders. PCP mixed with other drugs can cause the person to feel they are invincible, or make them think they can fly, or stop trains. It can make the user feel that everyone is out to get them, making them aggressive towards everybody.

STEROIDS

What are Steroids?

Steroids are manufactured testosterone-like drugs that are usually taken to build muscle, enhance performance, and improve appearance. Some steroids are used medically to treat many conditions including asthma, chronic lung disease, skin conditions and allergic reactions such as poison ivy. Non-medical use of steroids can have serious side effects. Using steroids for cosmetic or athletic purposes is not sanctioned in the United States.

Street names

Juice, Roids, Gym Candy, Pumpers, Stackers, Balls or Bulls, Weight Trainers, Arnies, A's or Anabolics

Trade Names

Anatrofin, Anaxvar, Annadrol, Bolasterone, Decadiabolin, Decadurabolin, Dehydropiandrosterone (BHEA), Delatestryl, Dianiabol, Dihydrolone, Durabolin, Dymethazine, Enoltestovis, Equipose, Gamma Hydroxybutilate, Maxibolin, Methatriol, Methyltestosterone, Parabolin, Quinolone, Therabolin, and Winstrol to name a few.

Method of Use

Oral tablets or liquid, or injected. Users take them in patterns called "cycling", which means they take them over a specific period of time, stop, and then start taking them again instead of continuously using them. Many users also take different types of steroids in combination with other drugs. This is known as "stacking".

Signs and Symptoms of Steroid Use

Steroid abusers often exhibit the following symptoms:

Rapid weight gain
Rapid muscle development
Acne flare up
Fluid retention
Yellow tint in the eyes and on skin (jaundice)
Mood swings, depression
Aggressive behavior
Premature balding

Drug Test Detection

Oral steroids will be found in your system up to several weeks after use. Injected steroids can be found for several months after use.

Short-term Consequences

Use of steroids can increase muscle mass, strength, and endurance, but can also cause liver tumors, jaundice, water retention, and high blood pressure. Some users show bad judgment because the drugs make them feel invincible. Other users suffer from uncontrolled aggression and violent behavior called "Roid Rage", or severe mood swings, manic episodes, and depression. They often suffer from paranoid jealousy, extreme irritability, and can have delusions.

Long-Term Consequences

When the body experiences a build up of steroids in its system, conditions such as hypertension, high cholesterol, kidney disease, stunted growth, brain damage, and heart damage are more than likely to occur. Women can experience irreversible deepening of the voice, shrinking of the breasts, menstrual irregularities, baldness and hair growth on other parts of the body, and genital swelling. Men can experience baldness, breast enlargement, sterility, shrinking of testicles and impotence. Steroids such as prednisone and other synthetic steroids can cause a rise in blood sugar by blocking the effect of insulin. Over time, users can develop diabetes.

DRUGS & ALCOHOL ON THE JOB

Alcohol and drugs in the workplace is receiving attention because of the public's increased awareness and concern about safety, productivity and health. Each year alcohol and drugs cost taxpayers billions of dollars in Federal Government drug-related expenditures. The National Institute on Drug Abuse reports that between 5 and 10% of workers are heavy users of alcohol. Furthermore, they report the following statistics about workers who use drugs:

22% of construction workers
16% of workers in the wholesale trade
19% of social services jobs
11% in manufacturing, retail and professional positions
26% in public offices [government jobs and government offices]

Most common signs to look for among employees are as follows:

Very troubled home life or family history.
Getting sick and having to go home a lot.
A lot of on going financial problems.
Isolation from the other employees.
Sudden communication problems, hard time communicating with other employees.
Will not keep eye-to-eye contact when talking to other employees. [At times]
Abrupt changes in the job attendance, quality of work, work output, discipline.
Unusual flare-ups or outbreaks of temper at other employees, high-strung, irritable, mood swings
Withdrawal from responsibility.

General changes in overall attitude, sluggish, slow reaction time
Deterioration of physical appearance and grooming.
Wearing of sunglasses at inappropriate times.
Continual wearing of long-sleeved garments particularly in hot weather or reluctance to wear short sleeves when appropriate.
Association with known substance abusers.
Unusual borrowing of money from friends, co-workers.
Stealing small items from employer, and workplace.
Secretive behavior, poorly concealed attempts to avoid attention and suspicion such as frequent trips to storage rooms, restroom, basement, to the bank, leaving suddenly to go to appointments.
Leaving the job for a few minutes in a very bad mood, returning a few minutes later happy and cheerful.
Being late for work, early departures from the job, regularly extended lunches

HEROIN & THE BODY

Heroin addiction is an addiction that often ends in death.

Heroin affects the body, the mind, and the spirit. The body will begin to wither away, muscles will begin to atrophy, and the user will not be able to ingest or digest food correctly. The mind will no longer function properly; the user will no longer make clear decisions. The inner peace of the heroin user will quickly slip through their fingers as they reach for more drugs.

Before the body is affected, the mind takes the first blow of heroin abuse. Immediately the heroin user can no longer view the world, the same way they did before the first dose of the drug. Paranoia will set in right off the bat. Following that is the obsession to acquire more and more of the drug. Towards the final stages of heroin addiction, the mind is so immersed in the addiction that the user can no longer tell right from wrong. The only way to reverse these heroin effects is through treatment.

EFFECTS ON THE BODY

Mind and Behaviors:	Mental clouding. Alters emotions leading to bouts of anxiety, sadness, and depression.
Central Nervous System:	Depresses activity. Pain sensation consciously perceived but not interpreted as pain. Slowly destroys central nervous system.
Heart & Blood:	Depresses heart activity. Low blood pressure. Possible cardiac failure.
Lungs:	Depresses breathing, pneumonia, and lung abscess.
Liver:	Enlarged liver, liver dysfunction, high incidence of hepatitis A, B, C, & D with shared needle use.
Kidneys:	Toxicity, kidney failure, inhibits urine voiding.
Bones & Muscles:	Infections including inflammation of the bone marrow, adjacent bone tissue and muscles.
Immune System:	May depress the body's ability to fight infection.
Other Risks:	Weight loss, edema (excess watery fluid), loss of consciousness, coma; potentially fatal, collapsed veins

Addiction
Abscesses
Collapsed veins
Bacterial infections

Soon after injection (or inhalation), heroin crosses the blood-brain barrier. Heroin is converted to morphine and binds rapidly to opioid receptors in the brain.

Medical consequences of chronic heroin abuse include scarred and/or collapsed veins, bacterial infections of the blood vessels and heart valves, abscesses (boils) and other soft-tissue infections, and liver or kidney disease. Lung complications (including various types of pneumonia and tuberculosis) may result from the poor health condition of the abuser as well as from heroin's depressing effects on respiration. Many of the additives in street heroin may include substances that do not readily dissolve and result in clogging the blood vessels that lead to the lungs, liver, kidneys, or brain. This can cause infection or even death of small patches of cells in vital organs. Immune reactions to these or other contaminants can cause arthritis or other rheumatologic problems. Of course, sharing of injection equipment or body fluids can lead to some of the most severe consequences of heroin abuse, infections of hepatitis B and C, and D HIV, and a host of other blood-borne viruses. Drug abusers can then pass these on to their sexual partners and or children.

SYMPTOMS OF HEROIN WITHDRAWALS:

1. Dilated pupils
2. Piloerection (goose bumps)
3. Watery eyes
4. Runny nose
5. Yawning
6. Loss of appetite for days
7. Tremors
8. Panic
9. Chills
10. Nausea
11. Muscle cramps & severe body pains
12. Insomnia for several nights

CHAPTER 6

THE PARTY DRUGS

SPEED

Speed is an amphetamine commonly used as a stimulant. Speed basically, makes your heart race and gives you a huge high and can keep you going for days. Usually found as a powder. Speed is a very common recreational drug and can be very dangerous for someone who has a weak heart or if you were mixing drugs such as Cocaine, ecstasy, or others.

Speed is also found in very low doses in such over the counter medication as Sudafed or other cold and flu recipes, which contain the ingredient Pseudoephedryne. The sale of large quantities of Sudafed can often be linked to underground speed manufacturers.

WHAT IT DOES

Speed increases your heart rate and your blood pressure and gives you a high. There are many side effects of taking amphetamines, which stem from the increased pulse and blood pressure.

The effects can last for 6 - 12 hours depending on how much was taken and the resistance already built up to it. Speed is highly addictive and as your body becomes used to it, you will need to use more and more of it to get the same high.

HOW IT IS TAKEN

Speed can be taken in either powder form, snorting it through the nose, or a pill, which is taken orally. When you use it, it causes your blood pressure and your heart rate to increase dramatically. You suddenly feel full of energy and everything seems more highlighted. You may notice uncontrollable trembling or movement in your arms and legs from the effects.

You may decide that the person sitting at the bar is your best mate or love of your life. You might talk all night long, at a million miles an hour, with no regard for reality. You may also find your entire body becomes either quite dry or you might find that you sweat uncontrollably.

SIDE EFFECTS

The main side effects of Speed are increased blood pressure and heart rate, dry mouth and nose, trembling and uncontrollable movement. Other side effects can also include blurred vision, light-headedness. The coming down from speed can be extreme and you may end up feeling like hell for a couple of days after a big night on speed. Hallucinations when coming down are also very common and you will pretty much have to put up with a few days of feeling like hell.

CAUTIONS

Speed found on the streets is usually not very pure. Somewhere between 5 - 10% of it is actually speed. The rest can be anything from battery acid to baking soda, and this can vary greatly. Because of this, a normal dose can actually vary in size, making you more at risk of an overdose.

If you have a weak heart or high blood pressure do not use this drug as the reaction can be extreme and deadly.

CRYSTAL METH

Crystal Meth is a very strong stimulant that can keep you going for days. It severely reduces inhibitions in people so they do and say things without regard for their personal safety or consequences. Originally, Crystal Meth was used by truckers and bikers to stay awake for long periods. It was made very popular in the US gay clubs in the 80's and 90's. Crystal Meth has been linked to an increased incidence of HIV/AIDS. Many people on it have unprotected sex because it totally takes away the need for personal safety.

Crystal Meth, also known as ICE, is like speed or coke on steroids, and even a small dose can keep you going for days and days. However, taking crystal meth is extremely dangerous and can cause coma and death even from a small dose!

WHAT IT DOES

It gives the user boundless energy, increases sexual awareness, and removes any form of inhibitions including safe sex.

WHAT HAPPENS WHEN YOU TAKE IT

You become highly energetic and almost manic in your behavior. The effects can last from a few hours for a very small dose, to several days for a larger dose.

SIDE EFFECTS

It causes increases in heart rate and blood pressure, which in turn can bring on a variety of problems. The side effects are very similar to that of speed and other amphetamines but are a lot stronger because of the strength of the drug.

CAUTIONS

Crystal meth is known to have increased the HIV/AIDS epidemic in the US as it reduces inhibitions in people and the need to have safe sex. For this reason alone, it is important to have someone with you who are "straight", not on drugs. Large doses of Crystal meth can be fatal as it causes users to lapse into a coma and then have respiratory arrest.

Never mix Crystal meth with other drugs such as alcohol as the reaction can be severe. Overuse can bring on paranoia, short-term memory loss, wild rages and mood swings as well as damage to your immune system. You would quickly develop a very strong, and damaging, psychological dependence on the drug.

COCAINE

This drug has been around for thousands of years. It is made from the leaves of the Cocoa plant. The North American Indians used to chew Cocoa leaves to get a high and have done so for up to five thousand years. Cocaine is a stimulant which increases your energy and lasts anywhere between 15 - 60 minutes. Usually found in white powder form it has been used medicinally as an anesthetic and was used in the original Coca Cola. Cocaine is highly addictive and has some very nasty side effects. Stimulants such as Cocaine, Speed and others can be fatal even in very small doses.

WHAT IT DOES

Cocaine makes users feel like they are the most important person on the earth and increases confidence and feelings of heightened wonder and importance. As the cocaine enters the bloodstream, it causes a rush or high as it spreads through the body, producing a mild numbing effect and general feeling of excitement.

HOW IT IS TAKEN

Cocaine, usually taken in a white powder form, snorted through the nose. Crack cocaine, which is chemically altered further, can be either injected or smoked. Injecting or smoking coke will increase the rush and make the high happen all that more quickly.

WHAT HAPPENS WHEN YOU TAKE IT

The initial rush comes very quickly and you will get a euphoric high quite quickly, however the high does not last long and will subside within about 15 - 30 minutes.

SIDE EFFECTS

Because it is addictive, as you regularly use cocaine you will need more and more of the stuff to get the same high. Side effects from cocaine can include nasal passage problems, if you smoke it can cause lung pain and lung damage. Because it is an appetite suppressant, coke can make users vulnerable to malnutrition, and like all stimulants, it can lead to heart problems. Injecting cocaine rapidly destroys the skin tissues and can cause ulcers.

Long-term use can result in a range of mental health conditions, from mild depression, to the extremes of cocaine psychosis, with symptoms similar to schizophrenia.

CAUTIONS

Cocaine has many unwanted side effects and is highly addictive. One of the more unusual side effects is that if a large quantity is snorted it can break down the cartilage in your nose, causing your nose actually collapse. Expensive and extensive plastic surgery will be required to correct this damage.

ECSTASY

Although it was never put on the market during the 1950s, the US Army did briefly investigate it for possible military applications as part of its chemical warfare program.

The most common party drugs are: Ecstasy/MDMA, methamphetamine, cocaine and speed. Studies are continuing into the long-term brain damage caused by the drug Ecstasy. In addition, Ecstasy users risk death by dehydration, heart failure, and or brain swelling.

STREET DOSAGE & ADMINISTRATION

The standard dose is approximately 80-150 mg, with the primary effects lasting up to four hours. Since the effects of the drug wear off quickly, users tend to take more of the drug and in higher doses. This leads to an addiction to it. In addition, when the drug no longer works as well for the person they advance to a stronger street drug. There is a greater chance of injury when the user has a history of heart disease, high blood pressure, or stroke.

WHAT IS ECSTASY?

Ecstasy is one of the most dangerous drugs threatening young people today. Called MDMA (3-4-Methylenedioxy methamphetamine) by scientists, it is a synthetic chemical derived from an essential oil of the sassafras tree. MDMA is also one of the easiest illegal drugs to obtain. Its effects are similar to those of amphetamines and hallucinogens. Distributed almost anywhere, it has become very popular at social events like raves, hip hop parties, concerts, etc, frequented by both adults and youths. While not all "event" attendees use Ecstasy, the drug often makes the circuit of these parties and can set up dangerous circumstances that can affect everyone there.

- Street Names: E, Adam, Roll, Bean, X and XTC
- Clarity, Essence, Stacy, Lover's Speed, Eve
- Form: Pills - usually white, yellow or brown
- Size, shape and design vary
- Pills are often branded with designer symbols

LEGAL OR NOT

First developed as an appetite suppressant in 1914, MDMA was used as a psychotherapeutic tool and started to become available on the street in the late '70s and early '80s. It was not until 1985 that Ecstasy was made illegal. It is classified as a "Schedule 1" controlled substance along with other narcotics like heroin, cocaine, and LSD. Penalties for possession, delivery, and manufacturing of the drug can include fines as high as $100,000 and up to 99 years or life in prison, depending on the amount seized.

DANGEROUS INGREDIENTS

One reason Ecstasy can be especially dangerous is the lack of ingredient content control. Ingredients are hard to get and manufacturers of the drug often use substitutes. They like to mix other harmful additives with the already dangerous mix. This practice is so common that "drug test kits" are often sold with the drug so users can test for purity. Because of the uncertainties about the drug sources, pharmacological agents, chemicals used to manufacture, and possible contaminants, it is difficult to measure the toxicity, consequences or symptoms that might be expected.

HOW IS IT USED

Ecstasy is usually taken in pill form. It also can be processed for injection. Some users are known to crush and snort the resulting powder. Others insert the pill into the anus where it is absorbed. This process is known as "shafting".

HOW DOES IT AFFECT YOU

Ecstasy is similar in nature to other amphetamines and hallucinogens. It speeds up the nervous system and acts as a mood enhancer. Also referred to as "the love drug", Ecstasy often makes the user feel good, happy and relaxed, at least at first. Contrary to rumors, Ecstasy is not an aphrodisiac, and can actually inhibit sexual performance. The taking of any drug affects people differently. Depending on the user's size, weight, health, dosage, and the other drugs being used, the reaction can range from mild to very severe. Anyone suffering from hypertension, heart disease, diabetes, epilepsy, mental illness or panic should avoid taking Ecstasy.

COMMON SIDE EFFECTS

The following effects start within 20 minutes of taking E and can last for 4 - 6 hours or longer:

Increased heart rate
Increased body temperature
Increased blood pressure
Increased confidence
Nausea

Anxiety
Feelings of well-being (happiness, love)
Sweating
Loss of appetite

OTHER REPORTED EFFECTS

Taking higher doses of MDMA will not increase the good feelings. In fact, higher dosages can cause convulsions, irrational behavior, and hallucinations. Users have reported having problems with insomnia, anxiety, paranoia, concentration and depression after taking the drug.

OVERDOSE

Taking too much Ecstasy can result in:
Extremely high body temperatures
High blood pressure
Hallucinations
Fast Heartbeat
Breathing problems
Death

Death often results from harmful overheating (hyperthermia), or from drinking too much at one time (hyponatremia). Hyponatremia is a condition where excess fluid intake swells the brain resulting in coma. A third cause of death is stimulation. Over stimulation of the nervous system can result in heart attack or brain hemorrhage.

WARNING SIGNS OF OVERDOSE

Feeling hot or unwell
Becoming confused, unable to talk properly
Headache
Vomiting
Not Sweating
Racing heart or pulse when resting
Fainting or collapsing
Loss of control over body movements
Tremors
Problems Urinating

LSD

LSD (lysergic acid diethylamide) is one of the major drugs making up the hallucinogen class. LSD, was discovered in 1938 and is one of the most potent mood-changing chemicals. It is manufactured from lysergic acid, which is found in ergot, a fungus that grows on rye and other grains.

LSD, commonly referred to as "acid", is sold on the street in tablets, capsules, and occasionally liquid form. It is odorless, colorless, and a slightly bitter taste, and is usually taken by mouth. Often LSD is added to absorbent paper, such as blotter paper. It is then cut into small squares; each square is equal to one dose.

The Drug Enforcement Administration reports that the strength of LSD samples obtained from illicit sources range from 20 to 80 micrograms of LSD per dose. This is considerably less than the levels reported during the 1960s and early 1970s, when the dosage ranged from 100 to 200 micrograms or higher per unit.

HEALTH HAZARDS

The effects of LSD are very unpredictable. They depend on several things, the amount taken, the user's personality, mood, expectations, and the surroundings in which the drug is used. Usually, the user feels the first effects of the drug 30 to 90 minutes after taking it. The physical effects include dilated pupils, higher body temperature, increased heart rate and blood pressure, sweating, loss of appetite, sleeplessness, dry mouth, and tremors.

Sensations and feelings change much more dramatically than the physical signs do. The user may feel several different emotions at once or swing rapidly from one emotion to another. If taken in a large enough dose, the drug produces delusions and visual hallucinations. The user's sense of time and self changes. Users report the feeling of hearing colors and seeing sounds. These changes can be frightening and can cause the user to panic. Users refer to their experience with LSD as a "trip", and refer to acute adverse reactions as "bad trips". These experiences, good or bad, are long lasting. Typically, they begin to come down from their trip after about twelve hours.

Some LSD users experience severe, terrifying thoughts and feelings. Some fear losing control, fear they are going insane, fear that they are dying, and or experience feelings of deep despair while on their LSD trip. Some fatal accidents have occurred during states of LSD intoxication. Users feel they can fly, believe they are invincible, or they might believe they are invisible so they go walking down the street in the nude. Users report seeing mice the size of large dogs, and birds that can talk, and pictures that move like a motion picture. Users, often carry on conversations with talking goldfish and invisible creatures.

Many LSD users experience flashbacks. These flashbacks are recurrences of certain aspects of a person's experience, without the person having taken the drug again. A flashback occurs suddenly, often without warning, and may occur within a few days or more than a year after LSD use. Flashbacks usually occur in people who use hallucinogens chronically or have an underlying personality problem. Otherwise, healthy people who use LSD occasionally may also have these flashbacks. Bad trips and flashbacks are only part of the risks of LSD use. LSD users may manifest relatively long-lasting psychoses, such as schizophrenia, or severe depression. It is difficult to determine the extent of the LSD involvement in these illnesses.

LSD is not like any other addictive drug like cocaine, amphetamine, heroin, or alcohol. However, the chronic use of many of the addictive drugs produces a tolerance of that particular drug. So many drug abusers who take a drug repeatedly must take progressively higher doses to achieve the state of intoxication that they had previously achieved. This is an extremely dangerous practice, given the unpredictability of the drug.

ADDITION INFORMATION ON HEROIN

Heroin abuse can cause serious complications during pregnancy, including miscarriage and premature delivery. Children born to addicted mothers are at greater risk of SIDS (sudden infant death syndrome), as well. Pregnant women should not be detoxified from opiates because of the increased risk of spontaneous abortion or premature delivery. Treatment with methadone is strongly advised. Although infants born to mothers taking prescribed methadone may show signs of physical dependence, they can be treated easily and safely in the hospital.

Why are heroin users at special
risk for contracting HIV/AIDS
and hepatitis B and C?

Heroin addicts are at risk for contracting HIV, hepatitis C, D & E and other infectious diseases. Often drug abusers are infected with HIV, and other blood-borne infections by sharing syringes that have been used by other infected individuals. They may also become infected with HIV or hepatitis through unprotected sexual contact with an infected person. Injection drug use has been a factor in an estimated 40 percent of all HIV, and more than half of all the hepatitis cases in the Nation.

By drug abuse treatment, prevention, and community-based outreach programs. They can eliminate drug use, and drug related risk behaviors such as needle sharing, unsafe sexual practices, the risk of exposure to HIV/AIDS, and other infectious diseases. Drug abuse prevention and treatment are highly effective in preventing the spread of HIV.

Heroin is a highly addictive drug and its use is a serious problem in America. Recent studies suggest a shift from injecting heroin to snorting it or smoking it. This is due to increased purity of the drug and the misconception that these forms of use will not lead to addiction. Heroin is processed from morphine, a naturally occurring substance, extracted from the seedpod of the Asian poppy plant.

Heroin usually appears as a white or brown powder. Street names for heroin include smack, H, skag, and junk. Other names may refer to types of heroin produced in a specific geographical area, such as Mexican black tar.

NOTE

As the person continues to use heroin they start needing more heroin to maintain the effects of this drug that they enjoy. They soon start selling off valuables for pennies on the dollar just to maintain their need for the drug. Then their use of heroin is no longer for enjoyment but to keep from being sick from withdrawal symptoms. Their good lifestyle they once enjoyed has now turned into just survival.

Soon after a single dose, the heroin abuser experiences the effects come and go in a just a few hours. After an injection of heroin, the user reports feeling a rush, accompanied by a warm flushing of the skin, and a very dry mouth. Following this initial rush, the user goes on the nod, a conscious but drowsy state. Mental functioning becomes clouded due to the depression of the central nervous system. Long-term effects of heroin appear after repeated use for some time. Chronic users may develop collapsed veins, infection of the heart lining and valves, and or liver disease.

Withdrawal from heroin may occur as early as a few hours after the last administration, producing drug craving, restlessness, muscle and bone pain, insomnia, diarrhea and vomiting, cold flashes with goose bumps and other symptoms. Major withdrawal symptoms peak between 3 to 7 days after the last dose and subside after about a week to ten days. Sudden withdrawal by heavily dependent users who are in poor health could be fatal, although heroin withdrawal is considered much less dangerous than alcohol withdrawal. If a person has been using heroin moderately the withdrawal symptoms may last about a week. They can be moderate to severe with some rough pain involved. A person that has been using heroin heavily for years will have major withdrawal systems for as long as ten to fifteen days, with severe sickness and pain. They will feel like every muscle and bone in their body is in pain.

Even though these withdrawals are very rough, with proper care and treatment during the detoxification process, this may be done with very little threat to life itself. There are other party drugs but not in use as much as the ones in this book. For more information on party drugs you, can contact your local detoxification unit, treatment program, or just use the Internet.

TRUE STORIES OF SURVIVAL FROM PEOPLE WHO LIVED THROUGH THEIR ADDICTION

My time in hell

By Walter V. Lee

I grew up being shifted from home to home, in and out of foster homes. My mother was a drunk and I knew who my dad was, but never saw him. I got through the eighth grade and left home being totally on my own at fifteen years of age. None of my relatives wanted me around at all and although my only sister was older than I was, she was too young to be able to take care of me. I traveled all over the country by thumb trying to find whatever a kid of fifteen could get in the way of work. I learned fast how to eat out of dumpsters and ask for chump change. I never really knew my mother at all because she did not raise me but she tried to take the credit for it. On my seventeenth birthday, I got my mother to sign for me to join the army. Here I started feeling for the first time in my life that I did belong somewhere. I also got started in my life of addiction at this time. It was not long and I was drinking heavy and using drugs at times.

After four years in the army, and one year of that in Vietnam, I was released from the army. I went to Salem Oregon, got married and tried to be the all American family man. My addiction to alcohol was getting critical at this point. I was not only having problems with my past catching up to me, I was having problems with PTSD (post traumatic stress disorder) from the Vietnam War. I soon realized that I could never be this all American married man and the marriage was over by the time I was twenty-five years old. I was drinking very heavily day and night seven days a week. I did not seem to care if I lived or died at this point. I was also using drugs whenever I could get them free. My life was reduced to a place in the bush for home and whatever little items I could get to try to make some kind of a home out of it. By the time I was thirty years old I did reach the third level of addiction.

I refused to accept any kind of help from anyone. I retreated to the mountains and live there for two years because I was very afraid of being around other people. This gave me a sense of pride because I was a survivalist and knew I could survive anywhere at all. Meanwhile life was plunging me deeper into depression, to the point where I felt like I was not even human. After two years, I left the mountains and came back into society. I soon found out I still was not able to be a part of that society. I could only watch from a distance. I would not let myself escape from the hell I built for myself to live in. I stayed this way until I was thirty-nine years old and met the one woman that could help me out of this man made hell I was living in. She did not pull me out; she gave me the opportunity to pull myself out. On August 20, 1989 at 6 AM I looked in the mirror and saw the sickest thing, God ever let live looking back at me. I threw the two joints in the toilet and poured the quart down the drain and I have been clean and sober ever since.

I started into recovery on August 20 1989 with nothing to my name but a couple holey blankets and the clothing I had on. Since that date, I have been through three and a half years of collage, certified as a rehabilitation specialist, licensed through the state, and now run my own treatment program. For many years, I have been reaching out to other Vietnam Veterans that are still in their own little hells. I am married now to a wonderful woman and we have a great seventeen-year-old son. We have been reunited with the children from my first marriage and are currently maintaining a good, stable lifestyle. I put myself in my own little hell and somehow I pulled myself up and out of the nightmare.

Walter V. Lee
Fairfield, CA. 94533

Tammy

I left home at sixteen years old. I am now forty-four years old. I was connected up with the wrong crowds at a very young age, about a month after I left home. I started getting deep into the alcohol and drugs, prostitution, dealing drugs and stolen property, and every other area of the drug scene. By the time I was eighteen years old I was deep into the world of addiction. I stayed into this evil, cruel, world until I was thirty-five years old. During those years, I was raped several times. It took me to the areas of life that I never knew really existed. At thirty-five years old, I entered a detoxification unit and started feeling for the first time the love that I had never felt before.

I soon learned that real love has nothing to do with sex or drugs. I was lucky I had not contracted any diseases and my body was still in good shape. I soon went into a long term inpatient treatment program and made up my mind that I was never going back. I had not talked to my family for many years when I called them for the first time clean and sober, it was very emotional. I started seeing the positive side of life in sobriety, and a better way to live. After I completed the inpatient treatment program, I got into an out patient treatment follow up program. Then I got a job for the first time in my life, and a place to call home, my home.

I could remember that as a child I had dreamt of becoming a nurse. I started studying a nurse and soon found out that I had more to me than I thought I did. I was working, attending AA and NE meetings, going to school, and working an internship for no pay at a local hospital. I had a real full plate, it was all positive, and I liked it. While I was still going to school, I began some dating.

One particular man that I had been dating for a while, who was also learning to be a nurse, became my husband. From the age of thirty-five my life started going up hill with complete positively.

Michael T.

I grew up in the slums of L.A. where life is infested with drugs, alcohol, violence, and death. I was in a gang by the time I was twelve, and had been using drugs since I was ten. I was on my own, and on the streets, by time I was fifteen years old. I had already started building my record with the law. Before I was twenty-three years old, I had already spent three years in San Quentin for stealing cars. At twenty-five I found I was positive for Hepatitis C. I stayed homeless and on the streets until I was thirty-three years old.

After my mother died of AIDS, I had nobody left from my family. I met an elderly man in Denver who trusted me enough to let me live at his home. This was the first time anybody trusted me in many years and it felt good. I started looking up to the man and he helped me change my life. I found I was enjoying going to church and AA meeting with him. I was also caring for and about this old man and found I liked to be needed. I also had a job and for the first time felt like I was somebody.

This old man died of old age and I cried crocodile tears for hours. On his deathbed, he had told me not to look back to only keep looking forward in life. He also told me, “I love you son”. This was the first time in my life any man had told me he loved me. I was thirty-seven then. I am forty-nine now and I have fifteen years clean and sober. I have a good job, my own family, and a future. God bless you and bless your life like he has mine

Mike

THE DEATH OF THE FAMILY UNIT & THE VICTIMS OF ADDICTION

THE CHILDREN

The family members of the addicted person are the victims of the addiction. Their problems are much more devastating than the problems of the addicted person. The victims of the addiction will suffer from the physical and mental abuse brought on by the addicted person. The mental abuse will be much more devastating for the children than for the mother. The children will have bad grades in school. Other kids in school will make fun of them over issues that they have no control over. They will be malnourished because of the shortage of food at home. This is because most of the family money will go to support the addiction.

As I have said before, the needs of the family are secondary to the needs of the addicted person. The children will suffer from low self-esteem and poor medical care. Another big problem the children will suffer is always having dirty clothing to wear to school because the money needed to keep their clothing clean has to be used to feed the addiction. They will find themselves never getting new clothing at all. What they will have for clothing will be old and out of fashion and other kids will make fun of them for this. Very poor dental care will lead to bad teeth and this will cause them big problems later in life. The physical abuse the children will endure will have a negative impact on them in school. Many of these children wish they were dead and may even start having suicidal thoughts.

Many of these children will only see a doctor when there is some kind of medical emergency. The mental abuse will lead the children to feel there is no use in trying in school because nobody cares anyway. They will find these children are fighting in school a lot because the other children are making fun of them all the time. Unfortunately, the schools seem to side with the children that come from the more well to do families. No mater if they are right or wrong, these poor children always seem to be wrong. They are much more likely to start using alcohol and drugs when they are young because of the negative lifestyle they have had to grow up in.

They always live in the fear of being homeless. Children are not stupid. They notice so much that goes on around them, becoming older than their years. The rent is not always paid because of the need to keep in drugs and alcohol. Yes, the drugs and alcohol come first over any of the household bills that need to be paid each month. These kids are real used to the law coming to the house or mom telling them that dad is in jail because of possession or a DUI. This has been going on all through their lives and seems all too normal to them. They grow up developing a very bad attitude towards cops and the law. These kids will not have their normal teenage years to enjoy because they will go right from twelve years old to adulthood. They go right from twelve years old to survival mode. Going to the hamburger joint and then to a movie with the other kids is probably something they will not get to do.

THE MOTHER

The mother will have most of the same issues the children have. Suicidal thoughts are out of the question because she feels she must be there for the children's sake. She may never have any relationships with other grown women. She is ashamed of the black eyes and bruises from the physical abuse. Her pride will not let her admit to another women that she is very badly abused. She will do without everything to try to provide for her children. She will do anything she has to do to try to keep some peace in the family and to shelter the children from the abuse. She will take beatings in order to protect her children. She will go hungry for days to let her children eat. She will go without medical care in order to let her children have things. She will try to hide some money every chance she gets to provide for her children. She may even try shoplifting.

She is in a situation that she sees no way out of. I have heard many people say there is always a way out. People that have never lived in this kind of lifestyle say, "There is always a way out". The abuser does everything they can to maintain total control over mom and the children. It is very easy to look in from the outside and say, "there is always a way out." She sees her family in a mental nightmare. She sees no stability in the family unit. There is no family pride at all. To her the family stays in survival mode all the time. The family isolates from other relatives in order to keep them from seeing what is going on. The violence within the family unit is daily and seems to a never-ending problem. The mother's greatest fear of her children starting to use alcohol and drugs soon becomes a reality. From dawn to dark, there is always a fear that hangs over the family. Everyone is afraid to say anything about it, so everyone acts as if everything is fine. The mother soon finds her children are getting completely out of control. Now she finds she is extremely fearful for their well being.

The legal problems seem be getting out of control and they keep moving all the time in order to keep out of reach CPS, child protection services, and the law. There soon comes a time in the physical and mental abusive life that she is living where she does not feel the pain of the beatings anymore. She may even start thinking of revenge now and start loosing her fears of him and his abuse. The mother may be thinking that legally she could end up in jail for assault. Soon her fears of ending up in jail seem to vanish. Someday soon, when the beatings start, the mother may mentally snap and all hell breaks loose. At this point she is acting on total terror and total rage combined at the same moment. With both these emotions at the same time, she is by no means in control of her actions. Any and everything she can get her hands on becomes a weapon and will used as one. The total terror and rage at the same time going on in her will not let her stop her assault on him. All the rage from all the years of being beaten will come out during these moments that seem like hours. All her adrenaline will be let loose at the same second.

If she has a knife, she may stab him twenty times. If she has a club, she may hit him twenty times. In her mind, she is going to do anything she has to do to stop the beatings and not let him up anymore. The law may call this murder but this is nothing but self-defense. It is easy for the District Attorney that has never lived a life like this to charge the mother with murder because he is blinded to the realities of a lifetime of physical and mental abuse. There have been many cases lately where the woman has been charged with first-degree murder, and the jury has found them not guilty due to temporary insanity. This tells me people are starting to see the reality of the terrifying lifestyle that some women and children are stuck in. In these court cases where the woman is charged with murder the District Attorney never wants the years of child abuse brought up because he knows they will loose every case. Most of these women's savage assaults towards the abuser are not only to stop the beatings on them, but in their minds, it is to save their children also.

All the above information is about alcohol and drug addiction and domestic violence. In eighty percent of all cases of domestic violence there are drug and alcohol addiction involved. In a time of war when a soldier gets kill crazy it is when total terror and total rage both engage at the same moment and their actions are almost just like actions an abused women goes through when she snaps. We give the soldier a medal but we put the woman in jail. There is something wrong with this picture.

THE DEATH OF THE FAMILY UNIT

The family members will try to do anything they can for many years to maintain the family and appease the one with the addiction. They will do without, go hungry, forget about any medical needs, and help to keep the addicted family members secret from everyone. The <u>mental stability</u> of the family is in shambles and stays at the point of total collapse. The normal <u>growth and bonding</u> of the family has never been established. The dog eat dog, watch your back, behavior becomes the everyday normal rule to live by.

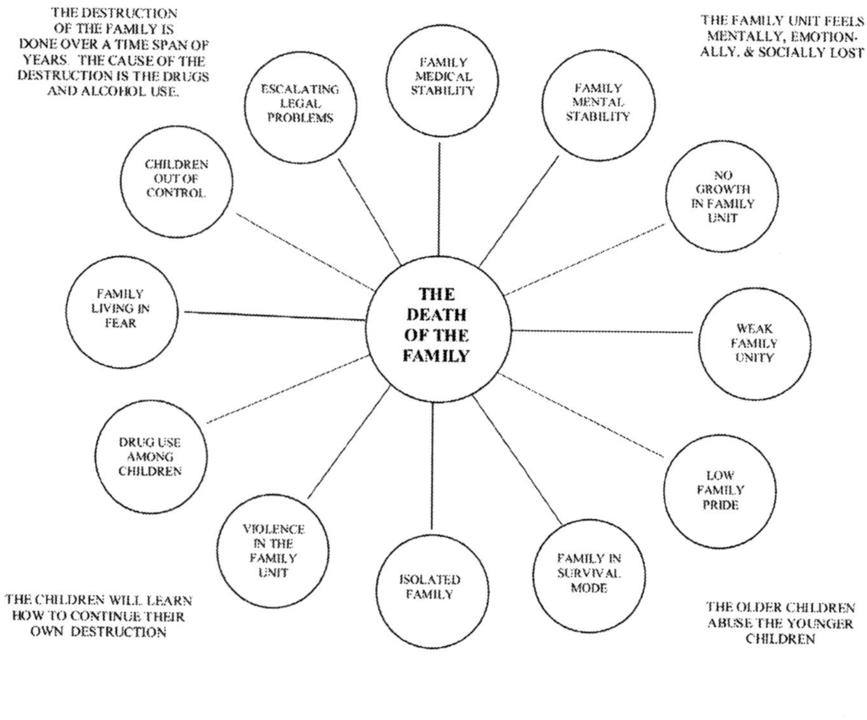

THE FAMILY REACHING OUT FOR HELP

FIRST THING, THE INTERVENTION

There are many resources in every county that can come to the aid of the shattered family unit and help them to become strong. The first thing that needs to be taken care of is getting the addicted family member out of the family and into the resources that can help them. There is a very positive thing called an intervention. An intervention is something that is set up by a certified, licensed rehabilitation counselor with all the family members involved. The counselor sets up the intervention without the addicted family member even knowing anything about it. It will be setup to happen on a night when the addicted family member in known to come home. The whole family is present and sitting in a circle with one empty chair waiting for the addicted family member. Once the addicted family arrives, all the family members get the chance to confront the addicted family member at once, one after another. This is not a finger-pointing event and it cannot be done in anger at all. This is when every family member gets a chance to tell the addicted family member how their addiction has effected them, what they have been going through, and how this all has made them feel. The family will have the addicted family member's bags packed before they even get home.

The counselor will start the intervention off by explaining to the addicted family member what is going on. The counselor sets it up for the addicted family member to be able to go right to detox as soon as the intervention is over. Every family member has their chance to tell the addicted family member all they have wanted to say, without any anger or accusative statements. The counselor steps in and offers them the detox and long-term treatment program. The counselor will tell them the detox is all set up for them to enter right now, tonight. The family members must all agree that if the family member with the addiction refuses detox and treatment, they will have to go and leave home right now, tonight. Unless the whole family agrees to this, it will not work. In most cases, the addicted family member does agree to go into detox and treatment. Once they really hear the pain they have been putting the family through it will have a big emotional effect on them. The long term treatment and after care will all be set up by the counselor. They will be totally in the hands of the professional people that can help them.

WHAT ABOUT THE FAMILY MEMBERS.

The first and most important thing the counselor will start working on will be the child or children in the family. The counselor will most likely already have a child counselor set up to start working with the children right away. The counselor has already been looking for any signs of physical or mental abuse. The counselor will than start getting the wife/husband set up with counseling, codependent group, group therapy, or any other services that might be needed to help stabilize the mother/father. The counselor will also start setting up resources like welfare, food stamps, county medical cards for the family, clothing resources, and any other resources they see that might be needed to help stabilize the family unit. The counselor's goal is to stabilize the family and help them to become strong and pull together as a family unit. The counselor knows the addicted family member is ok and being taken care of. Their main goal now will be to focus on the needs of the family unit. They will be working very close with the family, and all the resources that have been set up for them, to help them recover also. The family will be able to visit their loved one in treatment. They will also learn how to be supportive without being codependent towards them. They will learn how to pull together as a family and be strong.

WHAT HAPPENS WHEN THE ADDICTED FAMILY MEMBER COMES HOME FOR GOOD?

The family member must complete their long-term inpatient program and then their long-term outpatient aftercare program will be set up for them. Then they will come home and be under the care of the counselor that started the whole process several months age. The treatment for the rest of the family most likely will go on for a lot longer because of the severity of the effects the years of addiction had on them. The addicted family member must let this continued treatment go on and take however long it takes. The addicted person will have been well counseled on how they can be supportive towards their family still in treatment. The addicted family member needs to maintain focus on their recovery and continued treatment. The counselor will advise on doing things like getting a job and how to work and always keep up on their weekly support system.

A family can get these resources started by contacting any of the many treatment programs, detox units, county alcohol & drug services, county mental health services, or even the pastor of a church. You would be looking for a counselor that is willing to do intervention for the family. These counselors are available and can be reached by going through any of these services. You could get started by contacting AA or NA; they are listed in the phone book. Any detox unit can help you contact AA or NA groups.

WHAT IS SOBRIETY

Many people in early recovery, the first six months, will notice they are waking up in the mornings with a smile and a good attitude. They start feeling like they can focus on positive things in their lives now that the bondage of addiction has been lifted from them. These people in early recovery are still not out of hot water yet. They are very vulnerable to relapse very fast. Many of them will relapse several times before they can keep what ground they have gained, and keep on going, to develop a stronger sobriety. I have never liked the idea that if a person relapses they have got to go back to the beginning and start again. It is worth something when a person catches him or herself and gets back on track. Why should there be a punishment like having to start over, when a person has a relapse, gets back on track, and keeps going. A person's sobriety should be judged by the quality, not how much sobriety they have. The amount of time a person has in recovery or sobriety means nothing to me. The quality and strength of their everyday life tells me a lot about the person.

Over the years in this field, I have had many clients relapse and I have never told any of them they will have to start over. Them coming forward and admitting their relapse shows strong growth. I feel this should be rewarded, not punished. How can it be right to punish a person because they are human and make mistakes. When we are in recovery from addiction we are like children, finding our way in a new life of sobriety. I have always felt that in the long run it is better not to give relapsing any energy but instead pick up the pieces and continue to build a stronger sobriety in the long-run. This is not rewarding a relapse at all. This is just helping the person to learn by their relapse and helping them to go on in their life of sobriety. In life, we learn by our mistakes. This is the normal learning and growing process. We cannot grow in life without making mistakes. Sobriety is life to a person in recovery. I have a client that states, "I have two years of sobriety with one relapse." This is ok and he is back in school and getting straight A's. How can this be wrong?

One of the changes a person starts feeling in their early recovery is <u>financial stability</u> for them and their families. This is because the money is not being spent on alcohol and drugs anymore. They will start feeling a <u>positive growth</u> in their lives, and have a strong desire to better themselves. There will start being <u>family unity</u> and the relatives will start feeling this same unity also. The family starts working together to solve the little everyday family problems. Sometimes the family may need a family counselor to help get this family growth started. There will be a <u>pleasant happiness</u> in the person in early recover because they will start feeling their lives are going somewhere positive now. Within the person in early recovery and their families, there will be a <u>piece of mind</u> that will start glowing within the family as time goes on.

SOBRIETY COULD MEAN SOMETHING ELSE TO YOU. WHAT IS SOBRIETY TO YOU?

WHAT IS SOBRIETY

LIST WHAT SOBRIETY DOES MEAN TO YOU.

____
____
____
____
____
____
____
____
____

BY WORKING AT YOUR SUPPORT SYSTEM AND PUTTING YOUR RECOVERY, SOBRIETY, AND YOUR SUPPORT SYSTEM NUMBER ONE IN YOUR LIFE YOU WILL START FEELING THIS WITHIN THE FIRST YEAR.

TO THE PERSON EFFECTED WITH ADDICTION, SOBRIETY MEANS FREEDOM FROM THE BONDAGES OF ADDICTION

THERE IS HELP

HOW TO GET HELP & WHAT TO EXPECT

If there is a family member that is in need of help for their addiction there are services you can contact to get this help. Alcoholics Anonymous is known to do an intervention and help start the process. The next step would be to get them into a local detoxification unit. This is a place where they will stay for five to fifteen days to get all the drugs and alcohol cleared out of their system. The type of drugs they would be detoxing from will determine the severity of their detoxing process. Straight alcohol is easy because normally after the first three or four days they start feeling better and doing fine. There is one thing to watch for and that is alcoholic seizures. Not everyone has these seizures but occasionally they will find one person that has them. Counselors at detox centers are well trained. They know how to handle complicated situations. Usually people over the age of forty or so will be the ones in danger of alcoholic seizures. This is because of the many years of heavy drinking.

Heroin is a drug that most people feel is the hardest one to detox from because sometimes after three days the person is just starting to come down from the drug. When a person is detoxing from Heroin they will think every part in their body is in pain and some say they really thought they were going to die. I have never heard of anyone dyeing from Heroin withdrawals. The real fear of people withdrawing from Heroin is the ones that have been using Heroin and Methadone at the same time. Withdrawing from both these drugs at once can cause the person to die very fast. I remember one person that ended up in the hospital in intensive care for five days because they refused to tell the counselors at the detoxification unit that they had been taking Methadone along with Heroin. Other people that are watched are people that have been using heroin for ten to twenty years. Because of their long-term use, they will have an extra hard time withdrawing from this drug. It is not uncommon to see people very sick for ten or twelve days from withdrawing from Heroin.

Other complications that are commonly found in detoxification units are people with hidden medical problems. Many people use alcohol and drugs for twenty years and their bodies have been damaged and this all comes to the surface when they go into detox from these drugs. By the way, Alcohol is a drug also. Most of the time if there is a possible problem the counselor at the detoxification unit will send the person to get a full medical clearance if they feel there could be some medical problems. When they go to get this medical clearance the doctors will make sure they have any medication they may need for any newly found medical issues to take back to the detoxification unit with them. The counselors will make sure they take their medication on time. They will not feel like eating much for the first several days so most every detoxification unit keeps Cup-A-Soup on hand. Once they can eat, they will be well fed during their time in detox.

After the first or second day in the detoxification unit, the counselors start trying to get them into a long-term inpatient treatment program. Their counselors know every treatment program and most of the staff in these treatment programs, so they are sure they will get them in a program. If a person's health is to bad to detox in these detoxification units, they will try to help them get into a medical detoxification unit. This is because most all detoxification units are non-medical detoxification. While they are in the detox unit, they will start attending addiction rehabilitation groups. These are just regular groups. They will help prepare them for the more intense long-term inpatient treatment programs. This will also help get them more focused on treatment and what to expect in treatment. As their time in detox goes by they start feeling very good and they start thinking that maybe they can do this and stop this addiction. Their families will have their time when they can come to visit them while they are in the detox unit. While they are in the detox unit, the counselors are always looking for any signs of other possible problems or complications that could surface later on.

ON TO TREATMENT

Most inpatient treatment programs do not let the client have any phone use or visitors for the first three weeks or sometimes a month. They do encourage them to write letters during this time. There is a good reason for this. They must be totally focused on themselves and what they are going to be doing for the next four to six months. When they first get into the program, they will go through the normal intake process and orientation. Here they will get the whole run down of the program and what will be expected of them. They will also be able to express what they expect to get from the program. Any good treatment program is going to be telling their client the things they do not want to hear. It is important for these clients to be able to sit and listen to the things they do not want to hear. What they do not want to hear is just what they need to hear. There will always be people that walk out of their program because of issues like this.

In these inpatient treatment programs, the counselors will start helping the client learn a better and more positive way to live. Many programs offer daily living skills classes. Some programs offer money management classes because these clients knowledge of money management only goes as far as getting money and giving it to the dealers. These programs help the client to obtain stable living after they complete the program. Most all inpatient treatment programs offer their own outpatient treatment after care program that the clients can attend after they are back in their everyday lives. These out patient treatment after care programs range from six months long to eighteen months long. The longer the after care program is the better the client's chances are of maintaining a good life of sobriety. The biggest thing these people will learn is that living in recovery and sobriety is nothing more that being able to be who they were meant to be anyway. Drug and alcohol addiction distorted their natural skills and we were unable to use them for years. Going into recovery from addiction lets these natural skills come to the surface and start being used as if they were supposed to be all along. Living in recovery is nothing more than being able to be the person you could have been being all along.

HELP FOR THE VICTIMS OF ADDICTION, THE FAMILY MEMBERS

Once the addicted family member is well into treatment, the counselor will start working on the family members and start their treatment process. They will be meeting with the family members and setting them up with Counseling, BWA groups, Therapy, medical needs, and other local and county resources that will help to stabilize the family unit. They will set up the children with counseling if needed. They will help the family get into resources like money management services. The victims of the addiction will have a long healing process to go through. Addicted people in early recovery must let their family members take all the time they need for their recovery. As I stated in this book, one of the biggest problems is when the family member with the addiction goes home for the first time. When they first come home, they expect the whole family to be all happy and cheering for them with open arms and shouting with joy. When this does not happen, they will get all upset and wonder what is wrong. The family members are not ready to just give in and believe any of this yet. As far as the family goes, they could and most likely will relapse very soon anyway. Only time will help the family members to see and believe that he/she has really changed and will be ok. Sometimes this may take years so the addicted family member has to accept this and let change happen at its own pace, taking however much time it needs to take.

TWELVE DAILY THOUGHTS TO REMEMBER

Denial is a PRIMARY psychological symptom of addiction.

It is normal for the addicted person to be in denial of their addiction. Most of the time, the addicted person is the last person to recognize their addiction. They will continue their addiction to the gates of insanity, until their health is very bad, and ultimately to the point of death. Many addicted people will continue their addiction while their whole world around them collapses. Even to this point they will continue to blame everybody else for their problems and never be willing to look at their own actions. The addicted family member will use and abuse the whole family to maintain their addiction. Denial will overpower their ability to be reasonable and caring towards any family members.

The family is the victims of addiction

The severe complications related to addiction are by no means restricted to only the person with in the family unit with the active addiction. If the husband is afflicted with addiction, the wife will most likely be a victim of spousal [Physical & Mental] abuse. She may also be sexually abused on a regular basis. If there are grandparents living in the house they will most likely be victims of Elderly abuse, [both Physical & Mental]. If there are children in the house, they will become victims of child abuse. This covers a wide range of abuse. There is a lack of personal attention that children need every day. This attention never comes in a family unit afflicted with addiction. The children start doing thing to get negative attention because at least this is some form of attention. The abuse keeps getting more intense and could lead to a death in the family unit.

Cocaine on the human body

Cocaine/Crack has an overwhelming effect on the pleasure centers in the brain. The drug interferes, altars, and damage, and takes control of specialized cells that regulate pleasure, well being, and moods in the person's brain. Regular use of cocaine may shut off brain's ability to ever be or feel normal without cocaine. Long-term use will cause permanent addiction that will take a long time and a lot of work to break. Cocaine/Crack can damage liver's ability to detoxify blood, while reducing production of crucial enzymes needed for normal body functions. Hepatitis can be contracted and cause serious liver damage, cirrhosis, and liver cancer. Hepatitis is highly contagious and can be passed on to other. Cocaine/Crack can cause all the main blood arteries to constrict and cause major blockage in the main hears arteries causing heart trouble, heart attacks and death. Cocaine/Crack can cause problems in the reproductive system for men and women and could cause birth deformities. It will also cause increasing high blood pressure at a very young age.

Excuses for a relapse

Over the past seventeen years I have been working in this field, I have heard just about every excuse you could think of to justify a relapse. Most people that relapse had already planned the relapse. They did not just decide to relapse on the spur of the moment. Most of them will feed into their relapse beforehand on purpose to develop a good excuse. If a person is set on relapsing that means they went into recovery for the wrong reasons in the first place. The only real reason for a relapse is that you just do not want to stay clean & sober. Many people that go into recovery are thinking of the material gains they should receive from living a life of sobriety. When these material gains do not start coming in right away, they start thinking that this is not what I thought it was going to be. They have been in recovery for thirty days and, were is the new car, were is the great paying job, why aren't people giving me things?

The ten most common fears of sobriety

The ten most common fears of sobriety are not real at all but they are very real to the individual during the first few weeks of sobriety. These fears are brought on by our natural defenses and without the help of other that have already lived through this, they can cause major problems. These fears are The fear of **success and failure**, The fear of **change**, Along with the life of sobriety come the **fear of reality**, **Responsibility**, Fear of **obligations**, The **fear of yourself** is very simple, Fear of **facing your family** & relatives, **Legal problems** come with recovery, Fear of **rejection & acceptance**

Putting terms on treatment & recovery

Over the past seventeen years, I have tried to help many people to get into long-term inpatient treatment program. I have had many of these people try putting terms on their treatment. What I mean by putting terms on treatment and recover is, when a person wants to go into treatment and recovery but they are not sure they will to do what ever it takes to achieve recovery and sobriety. Many times when I would be talking about a certain inpatient treatment program for them the client would start by asking, "What all do I have to do there." This is the first sign of putting terms on recovery. They might say something like, "How many groups a day do I have to attend a day." They might ask a question like, "How long do I have to stay there." All statement like this is a strong indicator that the client wants to put terms of their treatment and recovery. "I will do this but I can't do this other stuff." or "I can stay in treatment for maybe a month but not 90 days." When a person is putting terms on treatment and recovery, what they are really saying is, "that they really do not want to stop using drugs and alcohol."

If you are the victims of addiction and abuse

If you are the victim of alcohol and drug related domestic violence, you need to start planning your escape right now. You do not have to stay in the dangerous situation any longer. The abuser will leave at times and will sleep at times. You do not have to do something that is going to put you in prison for the rest of your life.

Once the abuser is sound asleep, start calling and checking around with family, relatives, and old friends to find a place your children can be sent to in a real hurry. Do not say a word to the children about your plans because children have a problem keeping secret. You need to fine a place for you to go that you know the abuser will not be able to find you.

The two parts to a good weekly support system,

It is very important to remember that you must be active in both parts of the weekly support system. The serious part, the twelve step meetings, and the fun part, the coffee shop after meeting, clean & sober dances, AA camping trips, AA bowling teams, AA pot luck dinners and much more. The serious part is going to help you learn the tools you will need to stay clean and sober. The fun part is going to help you develop the lifestyle of sobriety and be socially connected in recovery. Get you family members involved in the fun parts of the weekly support system. It is so important to develop the lifestyle of sobriety along with learning the tools of recovery. Once you have developed the lifestyle of sobriety, you will be living without drugs and alcohol and it will feel natural to you. This will help to regain the family unity that you once enjoyed.

New in recovery, catch up on your medical needs,

Living through all those years of addiction means, you and your family may have some medical needs that need to be addressed. During our years of addiction, we let the medical, mental health, and dental needs of the family and yourself go un-addressed. You can get a medical card through county aid to pay for this medical care. It is not good to just say, "I feel ok so I will just pass on this", because you may have some hidden medical issues that was caused by the years of addiction. I am sure the children will need medical and dental attention that will need to be taken care of. Why not start your life of sobriety in good health.

Cleaning up old legal problems,

Just about everyone, entering into a life of recovery has some old legal issues to clear up. If your legal issues are very serious, you can get the help of a rehabilitation counselor that can help you through this. They can help you build a record of treatment, counseling, parenting classes, anger management classes and anything else that might be good for you to present to a judge that will shout the judge how hard you have been working. Most of the time, when a judge can see a person has been really working hard on their recovery, the judge gets real light with the sentencing. It will not be hard as you may think. Once you get these old legal problems out of the way, you will feel very good about yourself. You have nothing to fear by wanting to clear everything up so you can get a new start in recovery. Let the judge know that this is what you are really doing. You will be surprised at how much this will end up helping you.

Have patients & be understanding towards your family,

You cannot expect your family to be all happy, shouting, and jumping with joy because you have stopped the drugs and alcohol and went into recovery. Your family will not have much faith in this for a long time. It will take them months or maybe even years before they are ready to let their guard down and totally believe you are in recovery to stay. All these changes in the family will come but it will be on their terms and not yours. You must remember that your recovery is mainly physical and your family members recovery is both physical and mental. Do not start feeling bad thinking that you put your family through all this hell. The forgiveness must come from all family members and go to all family members.

Poor education, Poor job skills, Poor money management skills,

You can always take adult education classes to get your GED test. A good place to get information for this is at the local library. It does not hurt for you to get any kind of a job you can get for now, and start attending the local community collage, taking classes to get certified in a good field that you can make a good living for you and your family. It is recommended that you only take one or two classes a semester at first until you get into the swing of going to school. You will have a real busy plate for a few years but the results will be worth it. Even if you must work as a dishwasher while you are going to school, you can smile because you know this is only for a little while.

Remember, you will never be anything for anybody until you are first something to yourself. You must give your early recovery your heart, gut, blood, and soul in order for this to work. There are no putting terms on a good support system.

IN CLOSING

I have put my heart and all my knowledge in this book. I hope that it may shed some light on some families that are in the bondage of this devastating curse of addiction that has afflicted our country. I have seen many families torn apart because of addiction and I have seen many families re-united in the victory of recovery. They go on to live stable lives as a united family. Addiction is a curse that knows no boundaries or limits to its destructiveness. It has lead many people to imprisonment and death. By the grace of God and the people that have pledged their lives to working on the edge of the dark side of life there is hope. There is a way for these addicts to get the help they will need to pull themselves up and above the line of destruction and back to living normal productive lives. I am one of these many people who have pledged themselves to fight this thing called addiction and helping people who are in bondage to it. This book is dedicated to the people that played a big part in putting me in a position to be able to help people and families <u>from the darkness to the light.</u>

Bill Pillow
Arlyn Kjelmyr
David Svoboda
Tom Lucas
Eluese Coonie

Ira Brown

And above all, the ones, who stood by my side through it all,

My wife and my son, Chrystal and Christjan Huey.

I thank you for reading my book and hope it will bless you and your family.

God Bless you
Walter V. Lee

For $ 37.50, you can order a complete set of my charts & programs on disk. I use these in facilitating addiction rehabilitation groups. I have 40 programs & charts for addiction rehabilitation groups. If you would like to make an order please contact me personally at:

Yankee1@copper.net

About the Author

My name is Walter V. Lee. My wife's name is Chrystal M. Huey. I am an ADS Certified, CAADE Certified, and licensed drug & alcohol rehabilitation counselor/specialist. I have completed 3.5 years of collage and I have put all my knowledge and skills I have learned over the years into our book. I have been working in this field for 17 years and been the director of 2 treatment programs and a county shelter, and I have gained much experience from many other treatment programs. I have survived 20 years of addiction myself. I have been in recovery since 8/20/1988. For the past 11 years I have been the director of the ASAP Program, an outpatient treatment & support program for the Department of Veterans Affairs, Vocational Rehabilitation Services. Over the years I have worked with many clients and their families helping them to regain family unity living in recovery. When I first started working in this field it was taboo to try to help the family members of the addicted person. From the start of my career in 1990 I have always broken this unspoken rule and reached out to these family members that needed the help just as much if not more than the one with the active addiction. I was never one to stand with the crowd. I was the one always asking "Why or Why Not."

Printed in the United Kingdom
by Lightning Source UK Ltd.
127025UK00001B/217-228/A

9 781434 301840